FAMI

GW01463972

ULSTER GENEALOGIC.

Ulster
Genealogical
& Historical
Guild

VOLUME 2 NO 9
1993

incorporating Ulster Genealogical & Historical Guild *Newsletter*

Ulster Historical Foundation

12 College Square East

Belfast

BT1 6DD

ISBN 0 901905 61 5

Printed By Graham & Sons (Printers) Ltd.

51 Gortin Road, Omagh, Co. Tyrone

CONTENTS

LIST OF ILLUSTRATIONS

EDITORIAL

Much of the fabric of genealogical research is represented by the topics which feature in this edition of *Familia*. They include biographies of influential and interesting figures from the past, a study of the role of an important minority religion - Quakerism - and the value of gravestones as sources for tracing and identifying the migrant Irish. Of particular interest for the genealogical researcher, they all make exemplary use of a wide range of printed, manuscript and artefactual sources. In this respect, our aim is to provide, in addition to a good read, further encouragement to individual genealogical historians to develop their own researches and perhaps to submit their own source-based stories to *Familia* for consideration.

Trevor Parkhill
Kenneth Darwin

THE ELUSIVE MR OGILVIE (1740-1832)

by Flann Campbell

The Fitzgeralds of Kildare belong to one of the most documented dynasties in Ireland. Books by the score have been written about 'the good family', as the Geraldines became known, recording their dominance of the social and political life of the country. The names of the Great Earl of Kildare and his son Silken Thomas (not forgetting his five uncles who were executed at Tyburn) should be known to every school-child. There have been major studies of the first Duke of Leinster and his wife, Emily. No fewer than 1500 pages of correspondence of the Lennox sisters have been published, and fulsome biographies of the Locks of Norbury and the military Napiers have been written. Every twist and turn of the politics and romances of Lord Edward Fitzgerald, and his tragic wife, Pamela, have been recounted, and the mystery of Pamela's birth probed in a dozen books. We have been told a great deal about the lives of such contemporaries as Charles James Fox, Lord Castlereagh, Richard Brinsley Sheridan, Madame de Genlie and the third Duke of Richmond, and quite obviously there is no lack of information about the French Revolution, the 1798 Rising, and the Act of Union of 1800. The 'Pisan circle' in which the poets Byron and Shelly participated, and which has some connection with the Fitzgerald family, has been the subject of the most intense literary investigation since 1821-2.

And yet amid all these detailed records and accumulated research there is one person who was closely involved with the Fitzgeralds for more than 60 years, and who lived through many important events and knew many famous people in the late eighteenth and early nineteenth century, but whose own life and career remains something of an enigma. This was William Ogilvie who married the first Duchess of Leinster in 1774.

Who was this obscure school-master who came from nowhere to move into the highest social and political circles, was elected an M.P., and lived successively in several of the greatest houses in Ireland, England and France? How did a man who was certainly plain of feature, downright ugly some said, and reputedly bad-tempered, succeed in wooing one of the richest heiresses in the two kingdoms? How did he, in spite of ideological differences, captivate her son, Lord Edward Fitzgerald? Why were so many prominent personalities - among them the Prince Regent, William Pitt, Lord Grey, Horace

Walpole, Charles James Fox, Lord Clare, Sarah Siddons, Madame de Deffand, and the Dukes of Leinster and Richmond - willing to invite this apparent nobody to their salons or dining tables? What special endowment did this individual have that he could beget a daughter who would be painted by Sir Thomas Lawrence, marry a descendant of King Charles II, and become a friend of Mary Shelley?

William Ogilvie first appears on the public stage in Ireland around 1767 when appointed tutor by the first Duke and Duchess of Leinster. He was then 27 years of age, and reputed to have been born in Scotland. Certainly he had a strong Scottish accent, but he revealed little about his birth or origins. It was rumoured by his enemies that he had come over as a drummer boy in the army, and later had taught in a small school in Cole's Lane in Dublin where his salary was said to be £12 a year. When he endeavoured to raise this to 20 guineas he was dismissed, and decided to try his luck as a private teacher.

Ireland at this time was a deeply divided country. At the top of the social pyramid were the landlords, virtually all anglicans, who controlled economic and social power. This was the enormously privileged Protestant ascendancy. In the middle, and mainly confined to Ulster, were the Presbyterians comprising small farmers, medium farmers, merchants and manufacturers. At the bottom were the majority of Catholics, perhaps three-quarters of the total population, oppressed by poverty and penal laws. The administration was controlled by the viceroys and the 'under-takers' or powerful members of parliament who supported the government.

The Fitzgerald family, who had been converted to Protestantism in the early 17th century and thus had been enabled to hang on to their rich estates, owned two of the most magnificent mansions in the country, Carton in Kildare and Leinster House in Dublin. They might have been expected to subscribe to this pattern of wealth and privilege. However, they had always been prided themselves as being different from the general run of gentry and nobility. They saw themselves as Whigs who believed in parliamentary rule rather than the divine right of kings. They were also influenced by the liberal ideas of the enlightenment which was coming into Ireland from Britain and the continent in the 18th century. The first Duke of Leinster - described as a 'quiet, indolent, affectionate man' -regarded himself as a reforming landlord. His son was drawn towards the Volunteers and was proud to proclaim himself a 'patriot'.

The Duchess, whom he married in 1747, when she was only 15

4

years four months of age, was the fourth daughter of the second Duke of Redmond, who was a direct descendant of King Charles II and the French courtesan, Louise de Keroualle. Her first sister Louisa married Thomas Conolly, a long-serving member of the Irish parliament and owner of Castletown, a beautiful house near Celbridge in Co. Kildare; her second sister Caroline married Henry, later the first Lord Fox of Holland House in London; and her third sister Sarah married (after various emotional mishaps which included a brief flirtation with the future King George III) into the famous military family of Napier. By the prevailing social standards Emily was therefore extraordinarily well connected. In 1767 she was aged 36, and her husband was 45. They had ten living children aged from one to 18. She was a woman of stately beauty, of a lively natural intelligence combined with commonsense, and pleasant manners. Though brought up by governesses and largely self-taught, she was widely read and was regarded as an educated and cultivated woman.

In the mid-1760s the Duke and Duchess were both deeply concerned with the education and health of their numerous children, and after their eldest son William had been sent to school at Eton, they thought of employing a private tutor for the other older boys and girls. It was during this period that the Duchess - always a woman of advanced tastes - thought of inviting no less a person than Jean-Jacques Rousseau. The famous French philosopher, who had written *Emile,* a widely read book on the education of girls, a few years previously, was then living in exile in Derbyshire in England. Whether the Duchess ever actually wrote to Rousseau is debatable, but the intention seems to have been there. In the event, Rousseau did not reply. Would the history of Ireland have been any different if the radical Rousseau had come to Dublin at such a critical time?

The Duke probably knew nothing about the Rousseau scheme. A more conventional figure than his wife, he merely wanted a suitable tutor for his sons Charles, then aged 11, and Henry, aged six. The older girls, according to the upper-class fashion of the day, could be best left to governesses or servants. The man he chose, on the recommendation of a Dublin surgeon, seemed modest and orthodox enough. He was reputed to be a sound teacher of traditional school subjects. On interview the Duke is said to have been impressed, and promised the new tutor a 'handsome salary'.

The oft-quoted story of how Ogilvie first arrived for his job is told in Brian Fitzgerald's biography of the Duchess of Leinster: 'Emily was at Leinster House, entertaining Lady Leitrim, when the groom of the chamber came in and announced that the new tutor, Mr. Ogilvie, has come. 'Show him to his room' said the Duchess. 'Please, Your Grace is he to have wax candles or tallow?' the butler asked. Upon which Emily turned to Leitrim, and said in French: 'Qu'en pensez-vous?'. 'Oh! moulds will do until we see a little!'. Such was the introduction of Mr. William Ogilvie into the Fitzgerald family'.

Ogilvie was put in charge of the 11-year old Charles, a delicate boy; and then as he proved satisfactory to both master and mistress he took on responsibility for Henry (6), Edward (4), Sophia (5) and Robert (2). Sophia also had bad health. Four more children were born before 1773 when the Duke died. At first, the younger family lived mainly at Leinster House, but it was then decided for various reasons that they should move to an 'elegant' villa at Black Rock. Here they settled happily for the next six years. The Duke of Leinster preferred to stay at Carton with his older children, William (18), Emily (15), and Charlotte (8). The Duchess moved to and fro between the various houses, leaving Ogilvie in charge at the new villa.

Black Rock (two words in those days) was then a small seaside village about five miles from the centre of Dublin on the road to Dun Laoghaire and Dalkey. There were pleasant beaches nearby, and pretty views across the bay to Howth. Only a few miles to the south-west were the Dublin and Wicklow mountains. Black Rock was chosen because of the fresh sea-air, and the bathing which was coming into fashion for its curative health properties. Growing children could get plenty of exercise. The villa (which was later re-named 'Frescati') had been bought by the Duchess circa 1763-4. In spite of her sharing with her husband two magnificent residences, Carton in Kildare and Leinster House in Dublin, she seems to have preferred this modest house for its agreeable family atmosphere. It was surrounded by fields, woods and gardens, through which a small stream flowed. Eventually a tunnel was built under the main road to enable children safely to reach the sea-shore. The house, which remained in possession of the family for forty years, was small to begin with, but gradually several rooms were added until it became quite substantial.

Ogilvie soon made himself at home in these new surroundings. At first, he was content to teach the children what was appropriate to their various ages - Latin and Greek and French to the older boys, Mathematics to Lord Edward, English to old and young girls as well as boys. He was a good disciplinarian (though disobedience seems to have been rare) and made them rise early - in summer at about six o'clock - to get on with what he referred as their 'business', ie. lessons. He got on well with practically all the children, especially his favourite, Edward, of whom he wrote: 'His business is a pleasure to him yet carried on seriously and attentively ... I flatter myself that I shall be able to advance him very fast, imperceptibly to himself, as his little mind offers so much and retains so powerfully'. The other children in his care seemed to have been equally responsive if not always so bright intellectually. They did not seem to resent the fact that they seldom saw their father or that their mother came and went so frequently.

Underneath Ogilvie's gruff manner and dour appearance there proved to be both a shrewd mind and a remarkably kindly disposition. When he was finished with school-work the children could play and amuse themselves as they wished. Around the house and gardens there was always plenty of fun, bathing, cutting the hay, gardening, playing hide-and-seek or fishing for gurnets and mackerel in Dublin Bay. There were sailing expeditions to Lambay Island and excursions to town for tea parties or the theatre. Dogs and ponies were popular. They were all fond of the drama. In the evening there would be reading of stories or musical entertainment. All in all, it was a happy and cheerful time for both adults and children.

Ogilvie's second great virtue apart from teaching was that he could cope admirably with the many illnesses which afflicted those in his care. Health was the concern of everyone in Ireland, rich as well as poor, the upper classes as well as the common people. Smallpox was an ever-menacing threat, and tubercolosis widely feared. Even the simplest diseases such as measles and influenza were a major cause of suffering, even death. Children were especially vulnerable because of the ignorance of doctors and crudity of treatment.

The Fitzgeralds, though wealthy and well-educated and therefore not likely to be so open to infection, were not free from popular fears. Their correspondence is full of references to bowel movements, fevers, boils, skin eruptions, fractures, coughs and mysterious complaints of every sort. The Duchess, after all, had good reason to be nervous. She lost nine out of 21 of her live-born children prematurely, and was in a state of constant anxiety about her little ones. She herself (though it must be said that she lived to the ripe old age of 84) suffered from bad eyesight all her life, and frequently complained of the 'fidgets' (apparently nervous problems), 'feels' (emotional upsets), and the

'French ladies' (menstrual periods). Her husband died young.

Ogilvie seems to have had quite exceptional gifts as a nurse and amateur doctor. He believed firmly in the advantages of good food, fresh air, and exercise, and he often disapproved of current fashionable medical theories. If he thought it necessary he would send away the chosen doctor. At the same time he was open to new ideas about how infection was spread, particularly with regard to vaccination and smallpox. With babies and younger children he was as loving as any mother. There are many tales told of how he would sit up all night, bathing brows, singing lullabies, telling jokes, or reading stories to tiny boys and girls who could not sleep.

When the Duchess was away from Black Rock Ogilvie was expected to write almost daily progress reports. He undertook this task cheerfully, writing in formal language but usually in a chatty and informative way. His letters were invariably signed: 'I am, your Grace, your most obliged and humble servant, William Ogilvie'. A typical letter from the villa at this time ran as follows: 'All the dear children are just gone to bed and are all perfectly well as could be wished, and the happiest I am persuaded of earthly beings. It is impossible to tell your Grace how cheerful and pleasant they all are, but I hope you will share the pleasure next Monday as usual. All the dear boys are going vastly well, and with the greatest cheerfulness and spirit. The weather being so very good makes us a little idle now and then, but that I always look upon as so much gained on the side of Health which would make the first consideration'.

It was hardly surprising in these circumstances that the Duchess, burdened as she was with several small children and with a husband failing in health, found her tutor indispensible. In the beginning she was satisfied with his help as a teacher and nurse, but gradually she found that deeper emotions were involved. Lord Kildare, who had been made a duke in 1766, died of dropsy in November, 1773 at the age of 51. What was his widow Emily to do then? Could she manage her huge estate, two large houses, and the rearing of so many children? She was only 42 years of age, in the prime of her life, and still physically attractive. For more than a quarter of a century she had been accustomed to the companionsip of a warm-hearted and caring man. Now she was alone with so many practical responsibilities. In the person of Ogilvie, whom had been taken on as a servant, she found a strong sexual response, a sound intelligence, and a good character. The evidence does not point to the fact that at this stage, the early 1770s, they became lovers. Nevertheless, they grew ever closer in their affections.

Sometime during the first half of 1774, after a visit by the Duchess to see her brother at Goodwood, the momentous decision was taken by Emily and William that they should leave Ireland together, taking with them eight of the younger children. The reasons for this move abroad have never been fully explained, but it is clear that family's affairs had got into an emotional tangle. Ogilvie probably proposed marriage to the Duchess. She accepted, telling her eldest son, his grandmother and her sister, Louisa, but realised while she did so that there would be an ensuing scandal. The Irish landed classes all knew each other very well, and the most scurrilous gossip was likely to fly around the country. It was socially impossible according to most fashionable people for a duchess to marry a humble tutor. Matters were brought to a head in August, 1774 when the Earl of Bellamont - he was always called 'the Devil' by the family after this episode - was marrying the Duchess's oldest, daughter, also called Emily. Apparently there was an unpleasant scene at the wedding in which Bellamont insinuated that his mother-in-law was having sexual relations, possibly was even married, to Ogilvie. Malicious tales were quickly spread around Dublin, causing dismay to the new Duke of Leinster, who, after all, was now one of the most prominent figures in the country.

To escape from the scandal the family set sail for Waterford immediately after the Bellamont wedding. Their destination was Bordeaux. On board were the Duchess, Ogilvie, and Lords Henry, Edward, Robert, Edward and George, and Ladies Charlotte, Sophia, Fanny and Lucy. Their ages ranged from 16 to one year of age. The second oldest son Charles (aged 18) does not seem to have joined them until later. Accompanying the group were the servants Patrick and Mrs. Lynch and Dick Lawler. The eloping couple were married in October, 1774 in Toulouse by the Rev. Ellison who was a fellow of Trinity College Dublin. The service was in the Anglican rite and took place in an inn. The chief witness was the oldest daughter Charlotte (aged 16), a lively and intelligent, if at times awkward, girl. She kept a diary of the event.

According to her journal (which used fictitious names for the personalities involved: her mother was 'Stella' and Ogilvie was 'Davy') the decision to get married was only taken one day after breakfast in the inn. Ogilvie pleaded with the Duchess, and she agreed because of the opportunity provided by the presence of an Anglican clergyman. Charlotte wrote: 'The marriage ceremony was performed by Mr Ellisdon in the presence of Charlotte and Mrs. Rowley - the lovely Stella's woman. Stella was as beautiful as an angel. Mr. Ellisdon went away soon after. Charlotte wrote letters - and the lovely and adorable Stella and Davy spent a happy dear evening'.

The news of the marriage carried by Charlotte's letters to her aunt Louisa caused a sensation in Dublin. Old Lady Kildare took a tolerant view. Duke William was damaged in his pride, but suggested that his mother was the best judge of her own welfare. The gossip Mrs. Delaney said it was a 'wretched proceeding'. Louisa, who was invariably sensible, wrote perceptively: "You hurt your rank in the world, that is all you do: and if you gain happiness by it, I am sure you make a good exchange".

The next step was for the party of more than a dozen people to find themselves somewhere suitable to live. By marrying for a second time, the Duchess had given up her rights to the estate at Carton and Leinster House, but she was still well off financially with a jointure, or settlement, so long as she lived of £4,000 a year. The children also had capital or incomes. The decision was taken to move by way of Montpellier to the distant city of Marseilles where they rented a house for about eighteen months. Marseilles had a warm, dry climate, which was considered good for the children's health, but at the same time was open to contagious diseases brought in from Africa or the Middle East. In April, 1775 three of the younger girls, Sophia, Fanny and Lucy, were sent on the long journey to Bareges, a spa in the Pyrenees. Gloom was cast over the household when little Fanny, aged five, died on her return from Bareges. She had always been delicate. Ogilvie and his wife, however, were cheered up a few months later when a girl, Cecilia Margaret (always known as 'Ciss') was born to them. They had been married almost exactly nine months.

The ever-kindly Duke of Richmond, knowing of his sister's plight, then offered to lend them his chateau in Aubigny in the Berry region of France. After a long and tiring journey, described in one letter as a "vast moving", family and servants went through Avignon and Lyon up the Rhone valley and then westwards until they reached their new home in April, 1776. Richmond decided to travel over to France to see how they were settling in. His sister Sarah wished to come also but was prevented by illness. The meeting was emotionally fraught, but after some preliminary awkwardness the grand Duke and the humble school-teacher came to respect each other.

Sarah, who was undergoing her own marital difficulties at this moment, wrote to reassure her sister: 'My brother writes us all a delightful account of your family. In the first place, he likes Mr. Ogilvie vastly; he says that as far as he can judge he seems very sensible, to have very proper notions, and his manner just what it can be. In short, he seems excessively pleased with him, and says there is nothing he could wish otherwise in him but his Scotch accent, of which he has a little, and a little is too much'. In spite of the Scotch accent it was agreed that Ogilvie and the extended family should stay in the chateau for as long as they wished. Fortunately for them all they could not have chosen a more romantic place for their early years of marriage.

Aubigny was a small market town with a curious history. Situated halfway between Orleans and Bourges, it was in the middle of the Solange, a district of rivers, *etangs* and forests, famous for hunting game, shooting wild fowl, and fishing. It was drained by the rivers Nere and Sauldre, tributaries of the Loire. Founded in the gallo-romaine period, the abbey there had been associated with St. Martin de Tours. The town had been given the name 'ville des Stuarts' because of its long connection with the Darnley family of Scotland who had come out as mercenaries to help the so-called 'king of Bourges' who as Charles VII later drove the English out of France. Charles gave Jean Stuart land and forests in 1423, and for the next 250 years these were in the possession of the Stuart family. Jean was killed in February, 1429 at the siege of Orleans. A few months later the siege was lifted by Joan of Arc. It is possible that Joan passed through Aubigny on her way past Gien on the river Loire to see the king at Chinon. There is a house named after her in Aubigny. The fourth seigneur of Aubigny, Berault Stuart, began building a chateau in the new Renaissance style on the site of an old glass-workds about ten kilometres south-east of Aubigny. This magnificent building was named La Verrerie. It is now owned by the La Vogue family. The equally splendid chateau at Aubigny was rebuilt after a fire which destroyed much of the town. Fine gardens were later added by Le Notre.

The Stuarts held on to their estates until 1672 when the twelfth seigneur died without heir. There was then some dispute about who owned the property because King Charles II of England felt he had some claim to it because of his relationship with Henry Darnley, husband of Mary Queen of Scots. Louis XIV on the other hand believed that it was wrong for an English king to own a chateaux in France. However, he wished not to offend Charles whom he saw as a possibile political ally. The dilemma was solved by Louis agreeing that the estates should be given to Louise de Keroualle who had just given birth to a baby in London. The baby's father was Charles II.

Louise was born in Brittany in 1649, daughter of a minor gentleman soldier. She was a pretty, lively and intelligent girl, and in her late teens secured a position in the French court at Versailles. There she met the Duchess of Orleans, the famous 'Minette' who was the favourite sister of Charles II. Charles's wife was then seeking a maid-of-honour. The scheming Louis who was well aware of Charles's fondness for beautiful girls, and at the same time was trying to make a treaty between France and England against the rising power of Holland, brought Louise (aged 20) to Dover where the two kings met. Charles took Louise back to London, and soon transferred his affections from his established mistresses, Nell Gwynn and Lady Castlemaine, to the French girl. Louise held out against Charles for twelve months, but was finally seduced at Euston near the Newmarket racecourse in the autumn of 1671. She gave birth to a baby boy nine months later. He was soon granted the title of Duke of Richmond in the same way as Nell Gwynn's son was made Duke of St. Albans. Little did Ogilvie and his wife, newly moved into the Aubigny chateau, realise that within two years of their arrival there would be born to them a daughter who would link together the famous names of Richmond and St. Albans.

Louise was made Duchess of Portsmouth, and survived as Charles's favourite mistress until his death in 1685. However, as a Catholic and suspected rightly of being a spy for King Louis, her social situation was always precarious. Only her native intelligence and marked political gifts enabled her to come through the Popish Plot conspiracies of 1678-9 without harm. After Charles's death she persuaded his brother James II to give her and her son a pension. When William of Orange came to power she again showed her remarkable skills in intrigue by making sure that the pensions were continued.

Her son was taken to France by his mother, served in the French army briefly, and was brought up as a Catholic. In 1692 at the age of twenty, he decided to return to England, and became a Protestant. Louise survived until 1734, living in Aubigny, and turning to pious works of charity in her old age. She kept closely in touch with her grandson and his wife, and occasionally returned to England. She died at the age of 85. On her death the chateaux at Aubigny and La Verrerie reverted to her grandson who seemed more interested in building up his Sussex estates than he was in visiting France. It was the third Duke who in 1776 offered his sister Emily the opportunity to live in Aubigny.

The Duchess, with her gifts for home-making, and Ogilvie with his practical skills and shrewd judgement, soon began to make what was described in one letter as a 'pleasant, comfortable and happy life'. The chateau was large and cold, but they soon added to the furnishings which were already there, and lit huge fires to keep the place warm. In winter it was said to have required three cart loads of timber fuel every day. Dick Lawler, the coachman, was responsible for fetching wood, and Patrick Lynch and his wife were employed as house-keepers as they had been in Black Rock. Anne Simpson was the name of a nurse or governess they had also brought from Ireland. The Duchess kept overall control of the house-keeping, but delegated much of the detail to the capable Lynches as she had done at Black Rock. Ogilvie continued to act as tutor to his step-sons and daughters, and indicated, as he had always done, that he could steer them through any medical or emotional crisis. Physically strong himself, and mentally vigorous, he persisted in lauding the virtues of good food, and exercise in the open air, combined with plenty of schoolwork and reading. As he had shown when he was only a servant he now proved as a husband and father that he could be relied upon to nurse personally any child who was sick and ailing.

He got on well with most of the children, except for the independent-minded Charlotte who occasionally clashed with him. Both were said to have 'decided' and 'peremptory' views. The older boys, Henry and Charles, were often away in England or Ireland. Charles eventually joined the navy. Lucy was a warm-hearted, humorous and lovable girl who was referred to as 'comical' because of her pert ways. In retaliation she called her step-father 'Ogy', a name which became a family joke. Sophia was slow and easy-going, and rather plain physically. Apart from his own daughters, Ogilvie's favourite was, as always, Edward who was described by Sarah in a back-handed compliment as the 'least dull'.

When not occupied with his formal lessons, which were taken very seriously, Edward busied himself with gardening and growing flowers for which he had a strong taste. With the help of Ogilvie he built model fortifications on the estate, and as he grew older began to think of joining the British army. At that youthful stage he was an ardent loyalist, only too willing to fight the rebellious Americans. Edward was keen on riding, and regularly rode over to the neighbouring La Verrerie. If Ogilvie and his older brothers were away he liked to boast of himself as seigneur of the two chateaux.

In winter there was plenty of shooting and fishing which Edward and his step-father enjoyed. Even little Lucy was said to be fond of *la chasse*. During the summer days they would all go for long drives by coach or on horse-back exploring the countryside and small villages. In the evening they would chat together, play cards or chess, sing, or read books which were sent from England. Ogilvie would tell stories to the little children. From their mixing with local people they learned to speak a passable French. Edward in particular made himself a proficient linguist - a gift which he found useful in later years.

The main contact with the outside world was through correspondence within the family which, fortunately for historians, has been largely preserved. The Duchess, though many of her own letters have been lost, was a great collector. Her sisters Sarah and Louisa were superb letter writers - lively, chatty and informative. Though they often gossiped at length about trivial matters they succeeded in conveying much worldly wisdom, shrewd comments on political affairs, and the complexities of human relationships. Ogilvie himself wrote a strong clear, grammatical hand, usually filled with domestic details. In 1776 he had a long correspondence with Sarah about the children's health and the re-building of Black Rock. Two years later there were further letters about the possibility of selling the villa to the new viceroy, Lord Buckingham. A sum of £8,000 was mentioned but the deal came to nothing. The children, even the young ones, were encouraged regularly to put pen to paper, and they were scolded if they did not do so. Edward, who usually delighted to keep in touch with his mother when she was away, got so exasperated on one occasion that he said was 'kilt' with the writing. Both Charlotte and Lucy kept diaries as they grew older.

To keep in touch with wider society circles, and to stir themselves intellectually after their quiet rural existence, Ogilvie and his wife made several visits to Paris where they had excellent connections. The journey northwards took them two or three days' hard driving on poor roads. The Duke of Richmond had been British ambassador to France about ten years previously, and the Fitzgeralds were well known for their liberal views and artistic tastes. Henry and Edward also went to school for a short time in the French capital. They were all soon introduced to the social circles around the famous beauty Louise de la Valliere and the feminist Madame de Geoffrin. They were welcome guests in the noted salon of Madame de Deffand who was blind and over 80 years of age, but still celebrated as a hostess for writers and philosophers. The noted English blue-stocking Elizabeth Montagu visited Paris at this time. Horace Walpole, the English *belle lettrist,* was a contact between these people. In spite of his gruff manner and poor accent Ogilvie seems to have got on well with the *femmes/ savants.* His early introduction to the enlightenment in Ireland served him well when he was talking about the latest ideas of the Encyclopaedists. Rousseau's death in July, 1778 would have been a mutual talking point.

It was while on such a visit to Paris (probably in this case the journey was planned so that she could get the best medical attention in a big city) that the Duchess gave birth in May, 1776 to a daughter, Emily Charlotte, who is said to have been given the name 'Mimi' by a French maid. Judging by oblique references in letters there may have been miscarriages in 1776 and 1777. Emily was her last and 23rd child. She was then 47 years of age. On hearing this news Lady Albemarle, a malicious acquaintance in Dublin, told Louisa that it was shameful of the Duchess 'to pig again'. Aristocratic manners in those days could be very blunt. Ogilvie, of course, was immensely proud of his two daughters who had inherited their mother's rather than their father's looks. Mimi was said by Louisa to be a 'perfect beauty, with a fair complexion, dark hair and eyelashes. Surely nothing can sound prettier'.

The news which came through by letter or word-of-mouth that the married couple and their strangely assorted children were living happily at Aubigny finally persuaded the Richmond sisters that the time had come to withdraw any reservations they might previously have had about the marriage. Gradually, Ogilvie came to be seen, not as a fortune-hunter, but as a loving, intelligent and extraordinarily sensible spouse. Even the cautious Duke of Leinster learned to appreciate that the worst of the scandal was well behind them, and the Duke of Richmond made it clear that he could tolerate a Scottish accent so long as the person's other qualities were right.

Louisa Conolly summed up her views about Ogilvie in a long

letter she wrote to Sarah in April, 1780:

> For many years I thought all about his sense, his principle, and his attention to the boys; and finding so exactly what I wished I examined no further into his character. When he married my sister, I grew all anxiety to know ever individual part of his character, however, trifling. But the times were interesting to allow me so exact a scrutiny. And when I found he acted nobly, generously and disinterestedly in all that affair, I was satisfied. As to the attention and love he showed her, it seemed to be so, of course, in gratitude for her love for him; and that besides it was impossible for him to help adoring her, that I own that I did not see half his merit in his conduct. But now that the first violence may be supposed to be a little calmed, that people's eyes are not more fixed on his conduct now that a father and a master of a family it is natural for him to act in the most unconstrained way, not is the time to judge him, and to my excessive joy I am convinced that he is exactly I should have chosen for my sister; now I am perfectly satisfied and contented.

No doubt this realisation that Ogilvie's manifest virtues as a husband and father were now widely recognised was one of the factors which influenced the family decision to leave Aubigny. The original intention in coming to France had been to escape scandal, and now that this threat was diminished they could decide their future more freely. They had never deliberately planned to live abroad - it had been forced on them by circumstances. The circumstances had changed, and pressures were pushing them towards a return hom. Ogilvie was conscious of the fact that he had so far not been able to organise a career for himself. Possibly a job might be obtained in Ireland. He was also anxious to build up a dowry which he could hand over to his two young daughters. Edward was contemplating joining the army, and needed to make the necessary arrangements, preferably with the help of his influential uncle the Duke of Richmond or his older brother, the Duke of Leinster. Charlotte should really mix more in society and meet a suitable partner. The younger girls, Lucy, Cecilia and Emily required more stable prospects for the future.

But where were they to go - should it be England or Ireland? The first country undoubtedly had social advantages; the second could provide them immediately with a home, and the company of many friends and relatives. The Duchess could meet her oldest son and daughter whom she not met for several years. There were also new grandchildren to be seen. Moreover, at heart she did not approve of absentee landlords. Her sister Louisa wrote urging them to make up their minds. Regarding Black Rock, her advice was that they must either 'sell it, let it or keep it'.

In August, 1777 travelling by way of Dieppe and Brighton Ogilvie paid a visit to Sussex. Sarah was then staying at Goodwood, and took him on a guided tour of the neighbourhood. In May, 1778, that is soon after the birth of her last child, the Duchess returned to London where her portrait was painted for the second time by the most famous artist of his day, Joshua Reynolds. The picture portrayed a stately, handsome woman, still in her prime. On her way back to France she was involved in an adventure in which the ship in which she was travelling was seized by a French privateer. Fortunately she was not harmed, and got back to Aubigny with many tales to tell. In May, 1779 both she and her husband were back again briefly in London. Two months later, while apparently still in England, she made a will in which she left all her possessions to her 'dearly beloved husband' in the event of her death. The will, held in the West Sussex Record Office, Chichester, refers to 'plate, money, goods, chattels and estate' and included any annuity which may have been left to her by the first Duke of Leinster. It was never revoked and its tone indicates the extent of her feelings for her trusted 'Wm. Ogilvie'. In the summer of 1780 they left France and, by August, were back in Dublin.

It is not clear as to who took the decision to return to Ireland, but it must have been a mutual agreement, with the approval of the wider family. The choice was not an easy one as there was still some residue of the six-year old embarrassment caused by their elopement, and there were obviously many attractions to keep both adults and children in England. However they had a pleasant home waiting for them on the shores of Dublin Bay, and by this time it was plain for even the most biased observer to see that Ogilvie was a good husband and trusted father and stepfather.

These years at 'Frescati' (as the villa at Black Rock was now re-named) were among the happiest the family ever knew. The house was enlarged and made more comfortable. Thousands of pounds were spent on building new rooms and furnishing and decorating them. The gardens and woodlands were as much a source of pleasure as they had been during earlier years of residence. There was much entertaining, music at night, and the sharing of books. The old practice of reading aloud before the children went to bed was revived. Edward's passion for gardening - primroses, crocuses, violets, polyanthus, hyacinths, jonquils, pinks, narcissi, arbutus, roses, honeysuckle and lilac are some of the flowers mentioned in his letters - brought joy to everyone.

Ogilvie and his by now middle-aged wife were more deeply in love than ever. Their physical relationship seems to have been as passionate as it had always been, and their interests and tastes continued to be close. When separated they wrote each other the warmest of letters, with Ogilvie usually beginning 'My dearest angel', and ending 'Your most tenderly loving and affectionate W. Ogilvie'. Occasionally he would become quite poetical: 'I am really dying with impatience to see your beautiful face again, and to hug your lovely person in my fond loving arms ... to meet your warm tender kisses and to hang on your sweet balmy lips'. In one month (October, 1783) he wrote no fewer than 16 such letters. Gone was the old deference, and disappeared was the former reserve. As well as the love-talk, the letters were full of advice to the Duchess as to what she should eat, when she should go riding, and how she might best keep her bowels healthy. Her letters in reply have been mostly lost, but those which have survived were in the same vein. It was a tender marital relationship which survived until death many years later.

Ogilvie seems to have no difficulty moving into his expanded role as husband, father and tutor, and was prepared to intervene and give advice on every possible occasion which might affect his wife and extended family. There were constant references to his own two baby daughters, 'sweet Ciss' and 'pretty Mimi', and there are many appreciative comments about 'comical Lucy' and 'darling Eddy'. The older boys and girls, some of whom only stayed for short periods at 'Frescati', were encouraged to go on excursions to Dublin, to dinner parties and dances, or visit relatives in England. The discomfort and delays of travel by coach or sea were disregarded.

Edward continued to be the apple in the eye of both parents. His mother had always 'doated' on him, as she expressed it, and his step-father played chess with him, and told him what books to read. Together they planned new flower beds and shrubberies for Black Rock, and they often dined together, chatting about the family and the wider world. Ogilvie was always keen to give Edward advice about the numerous love affairs in which he got entangled as he grew older. Edward responded with praise for their productive meetings, constantly referring to the intellectual discussions they had and the mutual publications they read. In particular he welcomed the mathematics he continued to be taught when the opportunity arose. 'You know when I have a mind to study', he wrote, 'I never do so much good as when I am with Ogilvie'.

Edward was now in his late teens and thinking seriously of a career. Ogilvie and the Duke of Richmond wanted him to join the army, and the Duke succeeded in getting him a lieutenancy in the 96th Foot regiment. His stepfather gave him books to read about such military heroes as Julius Caesar and Alexander the Great. In December, 1780, only a few months after the family had returned to Ireland, he sailed from Ireland to the American wars, and was severely wounded several months later (September, 1781) in the battle of Eubaw Springs. Left for dead on the field, he was rescued and nursed back to health by a negro slave, Tony Small. Small became his loyal servant, and remained with him until Edward's death nearly 17 years later.

On recovery, Edward was posted to the West Indies, returning to Ireland in 1783 when with the help of his relative by marriage, Thomas Conolly, and with the support of his brothers Henry and Charles, he was returned as M.P. for the borough of Athy. Two years later, when he was aged 23, he went back to his regiment which was then stationed in Nova Scotia. He travelled adventurously in the North American prairies and forests, eventually crossing to the headwaters of the Mississippi and down to the Gulf of Mexico.

By this time Edward's views about democracy and the nature of society were beginning to take shape, and he wrote a long letter to Ogilvie about what he had seen among the white farmers and Red Indians of Canada. He was, as he said, 'deep into Rousseau', and he was all for the simple life, the equality of man, and by living only on what one produced from one's own labour. Writing to his mother in June, 1788, he said: 'The quality of everybody and of their manner of life, I like very much ... There are no gentlemen: everybody is on a footing provided he works and wants nothing; every man is exactly what he can make of himself or has made of himself by industry'. He did not refer to his native land, but it was clear from the context that he was finished with the privileges and lack of justice associated with the Protestant Ascendancy.

Ogilvie did not welcome such opinions about democracy, either at home or abroad, and hoped that they were the passing expressions of a youthful idealism. However, he himself was under growing pressure to give up his quiet domestic pleasures, and come out into the wider and more turbulent life of politics. Ireland in the 1780s was in a stage of rapid social and economic change. A patriot party led by Grattan and

Flood had come into existence which was working for some form of Irish independence; the Volunteers, who began as a defence force against a possible French invasion, had turned into a form of Protestant nationalism against British rule, and among middle-class Catholics there was the beginning of an agitation against the penal laws.

The famous Dungannon Convention of 1782 called for greater freedom for Papists. The mercantile laws which restricted Irish trade were ever more widely criticised. In the impoverished rural areas the Whiteboys, Steelboys and Hearts O'Oak boys were in their various ways violently questioning the supremacy of the landlords. For such Whig families as the Fitzgeralds these events presented a running series of challenges. It was all very well to be 'enlightened' but what practical steps should be taken, and which concrete policies should be adopted, as one crisis succeeded another?

Ogilvie, who was a wise man, well-read and accustomed to meet eminent politicians and the like, could not fail to be disturbed by such contemporary dilemmas. He was energetic and outgoing, and at that stage not content to confine his ambitions solely to his family. It was only natural that too much domesticity should occasionally pall on him. At first he tried to get some job or sinecure which would give him wider interest and simultaneously bring in some money. The Duke of Leinster hoped that he would be appointed Registrar of Deeds in Dublin which would bring in £1,300 a year, but this post was given to George Ogle, a loyal conservative M.P. Many years later he told his step-daughter, Charlotte, that he had been during this period offered an Irish peerage, but had turned down the offer because the Duchess feared she would have had to give up her own title for the inferior title of baroness. This was not true. He also said that he had regretted this refusal, and that those who professed to despise the peerage system 'were suffering from the language of jealousy and discontent'. This ambivalence towards a title was rather typical of his general equivocation towards matters of class-distinction and political reform.

In many respects his philosophic views - so far as we can deduce them - were broadly similar to those of other members of 'the good family', that is he was essentially a moderate, middle-of-the-road man, inclining neither towards radicalism nor reaction. On the constitutional issue he wanted more freedom for the Irish parliament, especially with regard to trade, but at the same time regarded himself as a loyal subject of the crown. During the 1780s he appears to have gone along with the Volunteers and patriots, though he did criticise Henry Grattan and the Bishop of Derry. If he had been a landlord he would have been much more a reforming agriculturist than a rack-renter. In England he was much closer to the liberals Fox and Sheridan than he was to the conservatives Pitt and Burke. His flirtation in France with the *philosophes* and blue-stockings were typical of one side of his nature.

On the other hand, he was willing to accept the financial and social advantages which came from his acquired status as a member of one of the wealthiest families in Ireland. If anyone could be described as upwardly mobile, he could. Like the overwhelming majority of his ascendancy contemporaries he feared democracy as a kind of mob rule. It is not clear whether he supported the American colonists in their struggle for freedom but he certainly detested the Jacobins who followed later. He did not think it illiberal (nor for that matter did his step-sons Henry and Charles and even the democratic Edward) to accept the parliamentary seat which Thomas Conolly secured for him in Ballyshannon in 1782. He was not a regular attender in the Irish House of Commons but he did make a long and closely-argued speech in May, 1787 when he attacked the mercantile laws for the way in which they restricted Irish trade. 'Ireland ought to be treated on a footing of equality', he said. This maiden speech (he never made another) was warmly praised by Henry Grattan. His sister-in-law Louisa was appreciative: 'He received the greatest applause ... he showed himself master of his subject, and expressed himself so well that he was listened to with great attention for an hour and a quarter'. Sarah was equally enthusiastic: 'It (the speech) is generally talked of as uncommonly good, full of information in the beginning and of fun in the latter part'.

If the conflict between the demands of public and private life became too acute he could escape to London where all kinds of temptation were on offer. The great palaces of Goodwood in Sussex and Holland House in London were open, and there were rich and powerful society friends there to entertain them. Ogilvie had by this time put his poor origins well behind him, and lost much of the gaucheness of his earlier years. His Scottish accent was not so obvious and, though he was still noted for his crumpy manner, he found that he could mix if he wished in the most fashionable circles. He was now on the most amiable terms with the Duke of Richmond who opened many a door for him in both country and town. His reputation of being something of an intellectual, as well as his considerable powers of conversation, stood him in good stead with Charles James Fox who was then at the peak of his political reputation. Ogilvie and Fox got on well, not only because they were relations through marriage, but because they shared some of the same Whiggish views. They frequently met in London. He also got to know Richard Brinsley Sheridan, playwright and M.P., and Horace Walpole, the essayist. Such famous people opened up a lively world to the poor Scottish dominie. On at least one occasion he was asked to dine with the prime minister, William Pitt, and he met the Prince Regent at the opera. He was introduced to King George III at a levee or royal tea-party, and found him 'tolerably gracious'.

A frequent theatre and concert-goer, both in Dublin and London, he struck a surprising but none the less warm-hearted friendship with the most celebrated actress of her day, Sarah Siddons. When invited he was only too pleased to bring Miss Siddons presents back from Paris. His wife did not resent these contacts but instead encouraged them. She was a very sociable person herself, enjoying company and conversation, playing cards at the gambling club Almacks and going to concerts and dances. To emphasise their superior social status, Lucy and Sophia were presented at court.

Travel on the continent was another diversion which appealed for reasons of pleasure and health. In the winter of 1786-7 they set out for Nice in the south of France, allegedly because Lucy was said to be ailing physically. She lived until 1851 so she cannot have been too feeble. It was while they were in that country that an event occurred which was destined to have dramatic long-term consequences for the family. In the spring of 1787 Ogilvie, Henry and Edward decided to return to Dublin for a meeting of the Irish parliament in which they served as M.P.s. The journey from Nice to Paris took nine days by coach, and while they were on the road they noticed groups of what seemed to be wealthy and important people journeying in the same direction. These turned out to be persons who were going to join the famous Assembly of Notables which was to discuss financial reforms in the state. It was, in fact, a prelude to the forthcoming collapse of the monarchy. On their way home through Wales they visited the famous 'ladies of Llangollen'.

The following summer they were back again in France, Ogilvie going to join his family at Toulouse - what memories of his marriage thirteen years previously that must have brought back - and the

Duchess going on a visit once again to the spa at Bareges in the Pyrenees. Edward joined her there where she was staying with Charlotte and her young children. Charlotte was soon to marry an English army officer, Col. Joseph Strutt she met in Spain. Edward had crossed Spain on mule-back, accompanied by his servant, Tony Small, from Gibraltar where he had been stationed. The family then set out together for two months' stay at Aubigny. They could not foretell, as they visited these familiar haunts and revived old memories, that the *ancien regime* was doomed, and that the French Revolution - which was to affect some of them directly - was just over the horizon.

The fall of the Bastille, in July, 1789, though at first its full significance was not appreciated, soon had repercussions in Ireland. The already deep divisions between the rich and the men-of-no-property widened, and the quarrel between pro- and anti-government forces became more acute. Conservatives drawn mainly from the anglican church (together with some upper-class Catholic laymen and clergy) were alarmed at the overthrow of the French feudal system, and feared for the stability of the social order and constitution at home. Their fears multiplied as the Terror got under way. Radicals, comprising many Presbyterians and the bulk of middle and poor Catholics were, on the contrary, filled with hope that a new dawn of democracy was at hand. Liberty, equality and fraternity when interpreted in Ireland could mean ultimately the fall of the ascendancy and the rise of the common people.

Ogilvie was caught in the middle of this political spectrum. The ambiguity which afflicted him as a member of a famous Whig family could no longer be avoided. By a coincidence, his 24 year old step-son Robert was secretary to the British ambassador in France, and happened to be in Paris when the Bastille was stormed in July, 1789. He wrote a long letter to Ogilvie describing the revolutionary fervour of the huge crowds, the dangers to the King, and the flight of the aristocracy into the country. He deplored the fact that supporters of the monarch were being butchered in the streets, and complained that 'the government of the town had become democratical'.

Ogilvie's response to this graphic letter is not known, but it can be assumed that he was disturbed by its contents and the other alarming news he was getting from France. He had spent several years in that country, and was well aware of the unstable nature of French society. His experience as an M.P. had also confirmed those long-standing opinions he held about wide social divisions in Ireland. His flirtations with the enlightenment and Rousseau may have tickled his liberal fancies so long as the new doctrines were in the realm of theory, but as soon as they threatened to become a revolutionary - and often dangerous -reality he must have hesitated. Radical ideas might be indulged in the mind, but to put them into practice was a different matter. In view of these pressures he decided not to run again the general election of 1791. He also began, along with his wife, seriously to consider whether they should stay in Ireland or not. The family had been happy in Black Rock, but their snug home was no longer such a safe place.

The precise date on which a decision was taken finally to leave 'Frescati' is not known, but it probably was between 1791 and 1793. This was a period of intense political activity affecting the three countries with which the Fitzgeralds were mainly involved. In France the King and Queen were executed, and large numbers of aristocrats guillotined. The British government declared war on France, and at home there was a wave of persecution against those proclaiming themselves democrats. Tom Paine was forced to flee from London. In Ireland the rebel Defenders became more active, and the United Irish organisation was founded. Protestant Volunteers demonstrated against the government in Dublin and Belfast. In the north the Presbyterians were steadily becoming more radicalised, and in the south the Catholic middle classes were strongly asserting their rights. Eventually the forty-shilling franchise was granted to Catholic as well as Protestant voters. In January, 1793 Edward Fitzgerald, who had just been returned for Kildare County, made a sensational speech in which he denounced the viceroy and his supporters in the Irish House of Commons as his majesty's 'worst subjects'. The same year three acts were passed which put even more severe restrictions on the democratic rights of the people.

All this turmoil must have been deeply disturbing to Ogilvie who, as we have seen, did not like being forced to take extreme positions politically. On balance, he was more a domestic rather than a public man, and in times of crisis tended to think first of his immediate family's welfare. The person who was causing him most anxiety was not the Duchess (who usually preferred to go along with what he advised) or his two daughters (who were still only children) but his beloved step-son, Edward. Edward had returned from the Americas in 1790, but not to make a suitable marriage or successfully pursue his army career as Ogilvie and his mother wished him to. Instead he entered a period of the most intense emotional turmoil and began to get involved in revolutionary politics. On reaching London he found to his consternation that the girl he had hoped to marry had wed another. He then had a brief affair with the wife of Richard Brinsley Sheridan who bore him a baby girl. Both Mrs. Sheridan, who was delicate, and the baby died soon afterwards. As for politics, Edward had been again returned at the behest of his brother, the Duke of Leinster, to the parliamentary seat of Kildare in the 1791 election, but he did not like what he saw in the House of Commons. Already what might be described as an advanced democrat and republican, he decided in the summer of 1792 to visit France to find out for himself what was happening there. He lodged for a while with no less a person than Tom Paine who had just published *The Rights of Man* and had to escape from England as a result. In November, 1792 he spoke at a meeting in White's Hotel in Paris in which he renounced all his hereditary titles. He dismayed Ogilvie by writing to say that in future he wished to be known as 'Le citoyen Edouard Fitzgerald'. In retaliation for this open rejection of the established order his army rank was taken away from him by King George. A short time after this event he was in the theatre in Paris and saw, and fell in love with, Pamela Sims, the reputed daughter of the writer Madame de Genlis and the Duke of Orleans. Edward and Pamela were married on 27th December, 1792 in Tournai, a small town just over the border in Belgium. This was a dangerous time. A few weeks later the King and Queen of France were executed. The terror was getting worse. A few weeks later the young couple were back in Dublin staying at 'Frescati'. It was then that he made his dramatic speech in the Irish House of Commons. Writing to his mother, he admitted that many respectable people in Ireland regarded him as now belonging to a 'nest of traitors'.

His sister Lucy was also causing the family much worry. Always individualistic and free in her speech, she worshipped Edward, and was influenced by everything he did and said. Still in her early twenties and not yet married, she increasingly proclaimed her sympathies with the most advanced democratic ideas. In London she walked in Green Park sporting green ribbons, and became known as the 'pretty Jacobin'. At Boyle Farm near Thomas Ditton (Pamela is buried in the local graveyard) where her brother Henry now lived and which had become the focus point for family activity, though willing to go to dances and have flirtations, she repeatedly quarrelled over politics, not only with her mother and step-father but also with her other more conventional relatives. In Dublin, where she was now in more or less continuous contact with Pamela, she was criticised for keeping bad (i.e. republican) company. At a ball she was snubbed and no one would dance with her because she wore her hair up in the French way. A friend remarked that she was really only 'Edward in petticoats'. Soon she was to meet, and be drawn emotionally towards, the United Irish leader, Arthur O'Connor.

There must have been many times during this era when Ogilvie despaired at the failure of the two step-children of whom he was most fond to follow his advice. All those years of careful tuition and moral guidance seemed to have come to naught. The happy days at 'Frescati' were all too obviously behind them. Politics and domestic stress were combining to drive them away from Ireland again. They had already bought a house in Grosvenor Square, London, probably as a precaution against more trouble, and they were now finally convinced that they must leave Ireland as a permanent home. In the early summer of 1794, after several false starts, they finally sold 'Frescati', and Ogilvie spent some weeks moving furniture, books and pictures. Edward and Pamela (who was expecting her first child) were offered accommodation at Kildare Lodge near Celbridge by Thomas Conolly, M.P., who lived with his wife Louisa in Castletown.

Abandoning 'Frescati' was a great wrench. They had been living on and off in Black Rock for more than a quarter of a century, and the villa was associated with all kinds of happy memories. Ogilvie, however, was now persuaded that, having apparently failed with Edward and Lucy, that he must pursue his parental role more successfully with his own two daughters, who were at an impressionable age of early teens. It was hoped that they would be much easier to handle because they were not interested in politics. To begin with, they were his own flesh-and-blood, and had been under his careful supervision since their birth. They had always proved loving and amenable, and they could not play the step-child ('You're not my real father and cannot boss me about') card in any arguments.

Cecilia was 19 when they moved to London, and eminently marriageable. She had already at the age of 15 and become engaged to the Marquess of Donegall, but he jilted her. She had quickly got over this disappointment, and was now looking for a husband. While riding on her brother's estate at Boyle Farm situated on the south side of the River Thames near Thames Ditton she met Charles Lock, a neighbour from Norbury Park near Box Hill on the same side of the river. Lock came from a family noted for its literary associations and liberal opinions. The novelist Fanny Burney and the French intellectual Madame de Stael lived at Norbury about this period. Unfortunately, Charles did not have much wealth, and the money-conscious Ogilvie went so far as to describe him rudely as a 'beggar'. He opposed the marriage, but was persuaded to change his mind. The young couple married in 1795.

Ogilvie's forebodings turned out to be true because Charles, though generous and well-meaning, lacked financial common sense, and tended to be idle. He hoped that either the Duke of Richmond would get him a job, or that his father-in-law would help with perpetual handouts.

Emily was nearly three years younger than her sister but just as eager to grow up and move into the rich social world which was opening up to her. Everyone had spoken well of her since she was a baby in Aubigny because of her good looks and amiable temperament. 'Pretty Mimi' was the pet of the family, and as she grew older her qualities became ever more appreciated. She was gifted socially, acquired a noticeably cultivated style, and spoke excellent French. Talented musically, she played the harpischord with her half-sister Lucy who performed on the harp. She was always fond of parties and dances, and easily adopted the *ton* of London society. A contemporary at this time spoke of her as a 'high beauty' with a 'charming manner', and reported that 'she makes conquests every day'. In 1796 she was painted by the eminent artist Thomas Lawrence. The portrait shows a tall girl, with delicate features and a fair complexion, masses of brown hair, and an elegant neck and shoulders. Her star proved to be happier than Cecilia's as she lived to make a good marriage, to bring up ten children successfully, and in her middle years to make friends with famous writers, including the poet Percy Bysshe Shelley and his wife Mary.

Ogilvie's hope that he could escape from the alarms of Irish and French politics and cultivate his domestic garden quietly in England was soon to be disappointed. Only a few months after leaving 'Frescati' he found his family embroiled once more in public strife. Edward by this time had gone too far down the revolutionary road easily to turn back. In spite of his love for Pamela, the birth in rapid succession of three babies, and the frequent exhortations of his mother, and almost all the rest of his family, he could not give up the cause which he believed to be just. He was often on the move, sometimes with his wife - the first born son Edward usually being put in care of the Duchess -and sometimes with his sister, Lucy, planning the rebellion which was seen now as inevitable and imminent. Lucy, partly living in Ireland and partly in England, became ever more deeply involved in these conspiracies. Her diary, though discreet when the occasions required, shows that she was as strongly committed to republicanism as Edward. Among some United Irishmen she was known as 'good Heart', a title of which she was proud.

In the spring of 1795, a new viceroy, Lord Fitzwilliam, came and went, leaving the people of Ireland more confused and oppressed than ever. In May Edward and his new friend Arthur O'Connor, one of the United Irish leaders, went to Basle in Switzerland where they met Lazar Hoche, the French general who was to lead an invasion force to Ireland. Pamela accompanied them as far as Hamburg where she gave birth to a daughter and met her mother, Madame de Genlis. A month later Wolfe Tone left Belfast for America. After a clash between Defenders and loyalists the Orange Order was founded at Loughgall in Co. Armagh.

The following year the intricate relationship between their public and private life became ever more complicated. Edward formally joined the United Irishmen, and in April, together with Pamela and O'Connor set out for Hamburg again, the two men to renew their military contacts, and Pamela to see her mother once more. On his way Edward took O'Connor to his mother's house in London where he introduced her to Lucy. She immediately fell in love with him, and was destined to pursue him emotionally for some years until she realised that he was not interested. During the summer Ogilvie went to Dublin on business matters. He had previously, much to the distress of his wife, had a violent quarrel with Lucy over politics. Her mother pleaded with Lucy to settle her quarrel, and this she did when she was staying at Castletown with her aunt Louisa. 'Papa and I made it up', she wrote in her diary. It was a curious comment on the times, and the peculiar relationships which were involved between the Irish upper classes, that on this occasion she went riding with Robert Stewart, who was emerging as one of the government's chief spokesmen and known to be an arch enemy of Irish nationalism. 'The Edwards came and the Castlereaghs and Papa' she wrote in her journal for 23rd October, 1796. And a few days later she reported: 'Edward and I walked to Carton and saw Lord Clare'. It would be interesting to know what these dedicated rebels and arch-Tories found to talk about amid the grandeur of Castletown and Carton.

In November, though he and Lucy had apparently been reconciled Ogilvie would not receive O'Connor when he made a social call to Leinster House where Lucy was staying. The fear of Jacobin infection was still too strong. The year ended with Edward and Pamela back at Kildare Lodge where they were joined by Lucy and O'Connor. They were looked after by Tony Small and a French servant named Julie. Tony and Julie later married. So contented were they all that Pamela described the lodge as 'dear, quiet, little, comfortable Kildare'. Whether Lucy and O'Connor were lovers is not clear, but they were certainly very intimate.

These four called themselves the 'Quoituor', and devoted themselves to a strange mixture of conspiratorial politics and domestic enjoyment. Lucy records in her diary how they spent one such day on 2nd December, 1796. 'Two men came from town, both great Democrats and very agreeable men. We spent a delightful afternoon divided between dancing and singing patriotic songs and the most interesting conversation; we sat up until two o'clock'. This comment was made only a few weeks before Wolfe Tone tried to land in Bantry Bay. The 'Quoituor' and their friends would have had much to talk about. Curiously, and to illustrate further how complex were relationships within the Irish upper classes, Lucy also mentions that a few weeks after they had been dancing and singing with democrats from Dublin they were visited by Lord Castlereagh and his wife. Was the soon-to-be-appointed chief secretary merely paying a social call or was he fishing for information? Again, what did they all discuss as they were drinking their tea or taking their sherry?

In 1797, after the French invasion had failed and the rebels had gone ever deeper underground, the political situation deteriorated further. Government repression became harsher, and the croppies were ruthlessly harried throughout the country. In February O'Connor was arrested while on an organising mission in Antrim, and Lucy tried in vain to visit him when he was transferred to a prison in Dublin. He smuggled out a message written to her in the flyleaf of a book. Six months later he was released. Edward moved to England briefly, and then returned suddenly to Dublin. Even the moderate Duke of Leinster was suspected of being not fully loyal to the crown. The teenagers Cecilia and Emily, who as we have seen were not at all political, were said to be hostile towards the King and the government. Emily, according to one report, was threatening to become a 'Charlotte Corday'.

The year 1798 opened ominously as the struggle between nationalists and unionists came to a head. The United Irishmen had taken the decision to rise in physical force against the crown, and were only waiting for the right moment to get French help. The government was trying systematically, and with the severest brutality, to break up the underground military forces, and at the same time intimidate all democrats and republicans. 'Croppies lie down' was the watchword in action as much as in words. The implications for the Fitzgerald family were frightening, as Ogilvie had forecast.

In March O'Connor, along with his fellow conspirator, the priest James Coigley, was arrested in Margate while on his way to France, O'Connor was later freed but Coigley was hanged. In Dublin, as though to show that they were no respecters of persons, the authorities raided Leinster House on a day in which Sarah, Louisa and the young Duchess of Leinster were present. Lucy was in a state of panic and desperation. The same month the directory of the United Irishmen in Dublin were arrested at a meeting, leaving only a few leaders, among them Edward, to carry on the struggle. A reward of £1,000 was offered for the capture of Edward.

Early in April, as the crisis got worse, there was a family council held at Boyle Farm in Surrey. Present at this crucial conference were the Duchess, Ogilvie, Cecilia, Emily, Lucy and Henry. A message was received from Pamela advising Lucy, much to her distress, not to come to Dublin. Henry, though not politically involved, indicated that he would do anything to save his brother. After long and, it must be supposed acrimonious argument, the decision was taken to send an older man as an emissary to Dublin where it was hoped that he would try to persuade Edward to escape as best he could from Ireland. The choice of Ogilvie for this dangerous mission showed how much they trusted his courage and good sense.

As soon as he arrived in Dublin Ogilvie went straight to the Irish Chancellor Clare who was a dyed-in-the-wool conservative but known to be well-disposed towards the Fitzgerald family. Clare received him sympathetically. 'For God's sake, get this young man out of the country', the chancellor is reputed to have said. 'The ports will be thrown open, and no hindrance whatever offered to him'. This was a repeat of the suggestion said to have been already made by both Robert Stewart and the viceroy, Lord Camden. But it was a futile

William Ogilvie - a caricature, Charles Lock (c.1800)

The Duchess of Leinster by Sir John Reynolds (1754)

proposal, showing how none of them had really come to terms with he strength of Edward's idealism.

The next problem for Ogilvie after seeing Lord Clare was to find out where Edward, who was on the run and constantly moving from house of house, was actually living. Only a handful of people, including Pamela and Tony Small, had this information. Pamela moved out of Leinster House after it was raided into a small lodging in nearby Denzille St. She was then in an advanced state of pregnancy and gave birth to a daughter while at this new address. On Tony Small's advice, Edward went to live in a friendly house in Portobello on the grand canal. It was owned by a person known as 'the widow Dillon'. There Edward met such comrades as were still at liberty, including the northern Presbyterian Samuel Neilson and the brothers from Cork, Henry and John Sheares. Edward toured Carlow and Kildare with Neilson to try and revive the military organisation which had been shattered by arrests.

Pamela's situation was a desperate one - she was not only emotionally under the most intense pressure but she could herself be arrested. She loved her husband dearly, and on no account would she let him down, still less betray him to the authorities. On the other hand, she now had three young children to look after, and in any event never had been a fully-fledged revolutionary. She was delicate and sensitive, and once again was supping full of horrors. Ogilvie, who had always feared her 'French' influence over Edward was now begging, perhaps bullying, her to intervene with her husband.

After much argument, Ogilvie persuaded her to give him Edward's address, and it was to Mrs. Dillon's house that he went to early in April. Edward received him with great emotion, but told him that he was wasting his time if he thought he could change his mind. According to the biographer Thomas Moore (who many years later interviewed the aged Ogilvie) Edward said: 'I am too deeply pledged to these men to be able to withdraw with honour'. The men to whom he was referring were probably the Sheares brothers who were in the house when Ogilvie called. On parting, Edward and his stepfather shook hands, and the latter gave the former a ring as a keep-sake. Ogilvie is said to have been in tears. They never saw each other again.

Ogilvie returned to London early in May, knowing that his mission had failed and filled with apprehension as to what was about to happen. He had good reason for his fears. Edward left Portobello, and moved to another house in Thomas St. where he hoped that he might be safer. Here on 19th May, probably betrayed by the informers Francis Magan and Francis Higgins, nick-named 'the Sham Squire', he was arrested after a struggle by the noted croppy-taker, Major Sirr. In the fight he killed one man, and was himself seriously wounded in the shoulder. The news of this incident did not reach London for several days where it caused shock and consternation. By then he was gravely ill from loss of blood and fever.

In London the family did not believe at first that Edward's wound was serious. Louisa Connolly, as always gallant and warm-hearted, wrote a letter to Ogilvie on 21st May which gave much detail about his capture, but implied that he was not gravely ill. Ogilvie replied immediately in two separate letters. There was more concern that the death of the raiding party member, Capt. Ryan, which might lead to a charge of murder. Consultations were held with such influential figures as Richard Brinsley Sheridan, Lord Grey, and Charles James Fox. The latter offered to go to Dublin to see what he could do. Meanwhile, Henry had decided that at all costs he must see his brother, and warned Ogilvie that Edward's fever was worse. As before, Henry proved to be strong and resourceful in a crisis. It was he and his Aunt Louisa who were admitted - in the strange company of Lord Clare - to prison to see Edward a few hours before he died. A vivid account of this dramatic visit to Newgate is given in the letter which Louisa wrote to Ogilvie on 4th June. The letter begins bluntly: 'My dear Mr. Ogilvie. At two o'clock this morning our beloved Edward was at peace'.

Pamela, who had been expelled from Ireland, along with her three children, the youngest only a few weeks old, at the behest of the government, arrived in London on 30th May, and was given shelter by the Duke of Richmond. Lucy reported that there was a violent altercation between Pamela and Ogilvie though she does not say what caused it. Doubtless Ogilvie held, unjustly it must be said, that Pamela was in many ways responsible for Edward's revolutionary activities. Lucy herself was distraught, particularly as both Henry and Pamela had persuaded her to stay in England. She records in her diary: 'My souls's treasure is dying and alone'.

In the meantime, several members of the family, not knowing precisely what was happening to Edward, but aware of the gravity of the situation, set out for Dublin. On the morning of 7th June the Duchess, having made some last pleas for help to the Duke of York and the Prince of Wales, took a stagecoach accompanied by her youngest daughter Emily. Two days later they arrived at Coleshill in Warwickshire, only to be overtaken by Ogilvie, Lucy and Sophia, who told them the news that Edward was dead. Sadly, they turned back to London, realising that there was no point in continuing their journey. The Duke of Richmond then took them all in temporarily to his palace at Goodwood. Here they met Pamela who was soon to go to Hamburg to join her putative mother, Madame de Genlis.

The government's wish for revenge was not assuaged by Edward's death, and the decision was taken - probably at the behest of Castlereagh - to sequestrate his property. This meant that his widow and her three children would be left penniless. Sarah said that the purpose was 'to strike terror into the heart of the disaffected'. Within a few weeks of the rebellion being crushed a bill of attainder was introduced of Edward and two of his fellow conspirators, who were prominent Protestant landowners from Co. Wexford. The latter were executed for their part in the rising. There were many protests at this vindictive bill which became law in October, 1798, partly on the grounds that Edward had never been put on trial and therefore could not be strictly classified as guilty. Charles James Fox said it was an "abominable proceeding", and Col. Napier, husband of Sarah, spoke of the 'illiberal rapacity of the prevailing faction of this miserable country'. The Duke of Richmond, Henry Fitzgerald, C. J. Fox, Lord Holland, Ogilvie, and later the Duchess herself petitioned the King. Lord Clare in a letter to Ogilvie referred to the 'poor little children'.

In 1799 Ogilvie applied to the Irish government for a reversal of the attainder, but was told by the new viceroy, Lord Cornwallis, that this would have to await the passing of the proposed bill to merge Ireland and Britain into one united kingdom. In fact, nothing was done for years. When the Duchess was dying in 1814 one of her last requests to her husband was for him to try and raise once again the question of the attainder. Ogilvie eventually purchased the estate out of his own money and shared it with Edward's son and his two sisters. Young Edward was then a captain in the British army. The attainder was finally lifted in 1819.

After Edward's tragic death his mother and stepfather were more determined than ever to leave sad Ireland, and settle down to what they hoped would be happier and more peaceful days in England. In March, 1799 the Duchess was staying with Emily at Holland House in London where a fellow guest was Charles Beauclerk, son of Topham Beauclerk and the Lady Diana Churchill. Topham had been the friend of Samuel Johnson, and Diana was the daughter of the third Duke of Marlborough. She was a talented artist. Charles is said to have come specially to the house to see Emily. It was an odd coincidence that both the Duchess of Leinster and Topham Beauclerk were descendants of King Charles II - the Duchess through the Richmond line from the French adventuress, Madame de Keroualle, and Beauclerk through the Dukes of St. Albans from Nell Gwynn. These rival ladies, Louise and Nell, had at one time been derided by a sectarian mob in Oxford as the "Catholic whore" and the "Protestant whore" respectively. Charles Beauclerk soon proposed to Emily much to the delight of both their families. Even the crusty Ogilvie could not disguise his pleasure. Their hostess, Lady Holland, wrote:

> My wishes have succeeded. Mimi's beauty and charming character have captivated Beau. He has obtained consent. Their settlements are drawing and their union will soon take place. Their dispositions suit exactly, and I never saw a fairer prospect than they have before them. She is uncommonly sensible, her temper is mild, and her manners serene; although cheerful, her turn is rather serious. Her person is lovely, her complexion a clear brown, black eyes, white teeth and a very small head, a fine shaped throat and neck, pretty hands and feet, and altogether she is as beautiful and fascinating as a woman can be.

The couple were married a month after they met at Holland House where Charles was said to be 'wild with spirits' and their closest friend Lord Holland 'jumps around the room with joy'. They went to live in Sussex where, as it turned out, they were neighbours of the poet Percy Bysshe Shelley. Emily proved to be almost as prolific as her legendary mother, and in more than 30 years of married life bore her 'Beau' four sons and six daughters.

The wayward Lucy also pleased her parents by putting the memory of her brother and her sweetheart, Arthur O'Connor (who by this time was in prison in Scotland) behind her. The tragedy of 1798 and the Act of Union which followed it convinced her that Ireland's cause, however noble, was a doomed one. Like some other rebels with similar views she found it difficuilt to sustain the idealism of her youth. Eventually she married Capt. (later Sir Admiral) Thomas Foley of the royal navy. They settled in Wales, and so far as we know she never went back to Ireland. She had no children. When her husband died she retired to the south of France until her own death in Nice in 1851. O'Connor, who had lived in the chateau of Bignon near

Fontainbleau for nearly half a century, passed away the following year.

Cecilia's marriage did not run so smoothly. As her father had forecast, her husband Charles Lock turned out to be accident-prone. He was offered a diplomatic post in Copenhagen after their wedding but for reasons which were not clear did not take it up. He was then appointed British consul in Naples, and went out there with his wife and children. They soon got into difficulties. At that time the ruler of Naples was the unpleasant King Bomba and his equally odious wife. Horatio Nelson was commander-in-chief of the British navy stationed in the Mediterranean, and was cohabiting with the notorious Lady Emma Hamilton (whom the Fitzgeralds described as a 'dolly'). Cecilia, through no fault of her own, fell foul of both the Queen and Lady Hamilton who were no doubt jealous of her youth and beauty, and spread rumours that she had Jacobin sympathies because of her relationship to Lord Edward. Charles made an even more serious mistake by alleging that the victualling of Nelson's ships was in the hands of corrupt captains. Nelson was furious and the young Lock had to go home in some disfavour. For three years he and his wife lived either at the Duchess's house in Wimbledon or at Norbury. There were frequent rows about money with Ogilvie who wrote one letter in which he admitted he was by nature 'stingy'. In 1804 Charles was appointed consul in Cairo, but in a long and circuitous route to Egypt he caught a fever and died in Malta. He was then only 34 and left a widow and three young children who were to be supported as best they could. No wonder Ogilvie got depressed at the failure of his early hopes and dreams. Cecilia, who was said by one of her contemporaries to have a 'passion for migration', later lived at various times in England, France and Italy. She died of cancer at Nice in 1824.

In the meantime, while their daughters' marriages were being made and unmade, and while new grand-children were being born, Ogilvie and the Duchess were seeking a quiet retreat in the country where they hoped they could spend a peaceful old age. In July, 1799 they bought a cottage in what was then the rural village of Wimbledon, and once again, as they had done in Aubigny and Black Rock, began 'to cultivate their garden'. For some years much of Ogilvie's still considerable energy was devoted to growing fruit, vegetables and flowers -an enterprise into which he put as much enthusiasm as he had previously done in the educating various Fitzgerald children or enjoying social life in London. 'My husband is working in the garden like a labourer', wrote the Duchess. 'Every day he is busy about a bit of ground where he is planting Potatoes, Carrots and Turnips and Cabbages, and is as eager about it as you ever see him about *anything* ... I am delighted about this, as it is such good employment, and employment we all want, but nobody such as him'.

To break what might have been this rustic monotony there were numerous visitors to the cottage, including Charles James Fox, who often came to lunch, and her son Robert who on one occasion arrived to stay with six children. Mimi arranged children's parties at the cottage, and Henry rode over from Boyle Farm. The Duchess's particular delight was her custody of young Edward Fitzgerald who was left in her care for many years by his mother, Pamela. As a young boy Edward was sent to a local dame school, and then in 1807 to Eton College. Later he joined the army. At one stage young Pamela, daughter of Edward, also lived at Wimbledon. The kindly but long-suffering Ogilvie wrote of his 'adopted orphans'.

Ogilvie believed that his wife needed more comfort and social life in her declining years, and in 1805 they bought a house in London's Grosvenor Square where they could spend the winters. Sadly this rural-cum-urban idyll which they planned was broken by the deaths of several members of the family. First, Thomas Conolly, husband of Louisa, died in 1803, soon to be followed by Col. George Napier, husband of Sarah. In 1804, as we have seen, young Charles Lock collapsed suddenly of a fever. Then in October of that year the oldest of the Duchess's sons, the Duke of Leinster, died prematurely at the age of 55. This was the eleventh of her children to predecease her. In 1808 Lady Diana Beauclerk died at the age of 73. The Duchess herself was beginning to show her years, but was sustained by the continuing health of Ogilvie, and the support and affection she got from her numerous progeny. At long last in 1814 she died peacefully in London in her 82nd year, loved and honoured by all who knew her. A warm and appreciative obituary was written by her daughter, Cecilia.

Ogilvie in spite of his advancing age - he was 74 at the time of his wife's death - was still full of plans and ideas. Not for him was a life of idleness or slippered ease. Surprisingly in view of the fact that he is said to have disliked Ireland (or more accurately certain aspects of Ireland) he had several years previously bought an estate in Ardglass, Co. Down, and had become accustomed to spend part of the summer months there. There are reports of his having been in Dublin in October, 1809 when his relative, the fourth Duke of Richmond, was viceroy there. Many years afterwards, when he was a very old man, he along with his daughter met the poet Thomas Moore in Dublin. Moore was writing a biography of Lord Edward, and wished to get what personal information he could about the United Irish leader. His book is dedicated:

> Mrs Beauclerk, this memoir of her illustrious relative is, with the hope that it may not altogether disappoint her enthusiastic feeling for his memory, inscribed by her obliged and faithful servant, Thomas Moore.

Mimi at this stage in her career had become very much a personality in her own right. She kept on good terms with her now elderly father, and her husband was tolerant and easygoing. She had successfully borne and brought up six sons and four daughters. However, as so often happens with women of her age, she sought a new freedom from the ties of domesticity. She was getting fat, but she was still lively and eager to make fresh friends. Certainly she was not willing to let her family inhibit her from involving herself in what she cherished most continental travel and the company of writers and artists. Circa 1820, when her father had settled down quietly in Ireland, she entered on a particularly dramatic phase in her career.

The year previously her sister, Cecilia, had been on a visit with her three daughters to Lake Como in northern Italy. There she had been entertained by the Irish novelist, Lady Morgan, who describes the various meetings they had in her memoirs. Cecilia then invited Mimi on to Nice where they were briefly joined by their father who in spite of his great age had wanted once again to travel to the south of France, a place which had so many happy memories for him. Mimi then decided early in 1821 to move on also with several daughters to Pisa. This town was then the centre of the famous 'Pisan circle', a group of young men and women noted for their radical politics and bohemian life-style. At its core were the famous poets Shelley and Byron, and round them were gathered several writers and hangers-on of writers, such as Mary Shelley, Lady Mountcashel, E.J. Trelawnney, Edward and Jane Williams, Claire Clairmont, John Taafe and Capt. Thomas Medwin. The lessers lights among them were to become celebrated because of their connection to Byron and Shelley. Three of them had Irish associations.

It is probable that Emily chose Pisa for her visit because she already had contacts with the Shelley family. At the beginning of the century the Shelleys had lived at Field Place, and the Beauclerks at

Horsham Lodge, both near Horsham in Sussex. Percy Shelley was acquainted with Lady Diana Beauclerk and was an admirer of her paintings. He had also visited Dublin as a young man, and knew well the history of Lord Edward and the Fitzgeralds. Anyone who was liberal-minded, morally tolerant about sexual behaviour, and against the English establishment was likely to please him.

Emily was made welcome to the magic Pisan circle for many other reasons. Her personality was lively and amiable, and she had made herself a good conversationalist, and well-informed on a wide range of subjects. At a lighter level she could gossip freely about the goings on of high society in England. If required, as she often was, she could give useful advice about the care and upbringing of children. This was especially pleasing to Mary Shelley who had recently lost two children, and whose son Percy was in poor health. The tense emotions of the various couples (Teresa Guiccoli was now living with Byron), and the constant anxieties of such individuals as Claire Clairmont and Mary Shelley herself, were often calmed down by the commonsense experience and practical approach of the older woman. Emily was very companionable and frequently gave dinner parties or dances for her bohemian friends. The adventurer Trelawny made some advances to Emily's daughter Caroline, who was then 18.

Mary Shelley's *Journal* contains several references to such social activities. 26th December, 1821: 'Medwin dines with Mrs. Beauclerk'. 25th January, 1821: 'Go to Mrs. Beaclerc's in the evening'. 7th February, 1822: 'Read Homer, Tacitus and 'Emile'. Shelley and Edward depart from La Spezzia. Walk with Jane (Williams) and to the opera with her in the evening. With E. Trelawny afterwards to Mrs. Beaclerc's ball'. 2nd March, 1822: 'Read Homer. Walk with Jane. Spend evening at Mrs. Beauclerc's'.

Lord Byron was at first glad to welcome anyone who was related to his hero, Lord Edward Fitzgerald, and could speak with experience of the events of 1798. Later, he turned against Mimi when she apparently failed to greet him warmly enough at her house. He suspected her (probably rightly) of gossiping too freely about his attitude towards Claire Clairmont and her daughter Allegra. Both Mimi and Mrs. Mason tried unsuccessfully to intervene in this very tense situation before Allegra died of a fever. Edward Williams (who was drowned with Shelley in July, 1821) commented on Byron's sarcasm towards Mimi:

There is a Mrs. B(eauclerk) here with a litter of seven (sic) daughters, she is the gayest lady, and the only one who gives dances, for the young squaws are arriving at that age when as Lord Byron says they must waltz for their livelihood.

Lady Mountcashel, who was living in anonymity with her Irish lover, George Tighe, assumed the name 'Mrs. Mason' which she had taken from a novel written by her former governess, the feminist Mary Wollstonecraft (and, of course, the mother of Mary Shelley). She is referred to as 'Minerva' in the various journals because of her wisdom, and she had a particularly strong influence on Claire Clairmont through some of the most traumatic incidents in the latter's life. Mrs. Mason added a further Irish dimension because she was an advanced liberal, believed in the emancipation of women, and had had some connections with the United Irishmen. When Lord Edward had been hiding in 1798 she had given shelter to his wife, Pamela. Another person with Irish connections involved in the circle was John Taafe who had come to Italy in 1815. He was something of a man of mystery.

Claire Clairmont was a source of friction within the group as she was admired by the Shelleys but Byron resented the fact that she was pursuing him after their initial intimacy in England and Switzerland had been broken off. They had also quarrelled when their daughter, Allegra, had been put in an Italian convent against her mother's wishes. During 1820-1 she moved from city to city in northern Italy where on a number of occasions she met Emily in Ravenna, Florence, Pisa and Livorno. No doubt she found the older woman's help and advice encouraging though it did not assist her relationships with her former lover. In later years when they returned to England Claire, along with Mary Shelley, was a close friend of Emily's son, George.

Capt. Thomas Medwin, who was a cousin of Shelley, lived near him when a boy in Sussex, and went to the same preparatory school as the poet, was a particular admirer of Emily. 'No one from her intercourse with the great world', and the leading personages of her time', he wrote 'had a more copious fund of anecdote. She was indeed a person of first-rate talents and acquirements, possessed an *esprit de societe* quite unique, and her house which she opened every evening was a first-rate resource'.

The individual from this complicated menage of poets and bohemians, rebels and feminists, who established the most permanent relationships with the Beauclerks during this hectic period was Mary Shelley who was constantly worried not only about her husband's happiness but also about the health of her sickly child, Percy. A baby son and a baby daughter had recently died in tragic circumstances. Mary herself was still only in her early twenties. She had a fevered imagination out of which she had just written the horror novel *Frankenstein*. Emily had learnt much from that shrewd old doctor, William Ogilvie, and knew a great deal about bringing up children. Mary could rely upon her for sensible advice about both child health as well as adult emotions. Sadly Emily was not in Pisa when her help was most needed.

Emily seems to have left Italy in April, 1822, that is three months before Shelley and Edward Williams were so tragically drowned in the Bay of Livorno. She thus escaped the immediate impact of the disaster but, probably heard of it on her way back to England. Later came the news that Byron had died in Greece. The Italian idyll was well and truly over.

When Mary got back to England in 1823 she quickly resumed contact with the Beauclerk parents and children, and for more than two decades they remained on the closest terms. There was a constant criss-crossing of the lives of old friends, including Claire Clairmont, until death cut them short. Mary was always made welcome in the Sussex home of Emily and her husband, and there were emotional - if not necessarily sexual - involvements with at least three of the children. Both generations had much in common - they were inclined toward radicalism in politics, deeply involved with art and literature, and had personalities which were sympathetic to each other.

Mary was a close confidante of Georgina ('Gee') Beauclerk whom she had known as a teenager in Pisa, and she helped her through a sensational divorce case against her husband Dean Paul in 1831. She was also involved closely with the oldest son, Aubrey William, and it is assumed that he was the 'A.B.' to whom she refers often and affectionately in her *Journals*. Aubrey, like his father before him, was briefly a member of the British House of Commons. He was well known for his progressive views, which included the abolition of slavery, the reform of the established church, and the ending of the tithe system. Claire Clairmont, who had recently returned from her exile as a governess in Russia, came into the picture again when she, along with Mary, helped Aubrey through a series of illnesses. His brother George Robert, the third Beauclerk son, who eventually after the death of Aubrey inherited the Ogilvie estate in Ireland, was another friend of Mary's. He was a radical M.P. for East Surrey in the

1840s.

While all this high literary drama was taking place, involving his daughter and some of his grandchildren, Ogilvie was busy trying to re-start a new life in Ireland. Though now in his eighties, he had in the early 1820s another ten years to live, and he planned to devote what energies he had left to the building up of the estate which he had bought from his step-son Charles in 1806. This was in the remote village of Ardglass in Co. Down, and consisted of a large demesne of between 3,000 and 4,000 acres and several run-down buildings. The property had been in the hands of the Fitzgerald family through marriage since the days of Henry VII. It had been left to Charles, 3rd son of the first Duke of Leinster, by his mother. Charles had served in the royal navy, and for some years had been a M.P. in the Irish House of Commons. He was created Baron Lecale (the local name of the district in Co. Down) in 1800 for his services in getting the Act of Union passed. Ogilvie paid £26,000 for the estate which was a large sum of money in those days. It is not clear where he got the money, but it must have been saved from his wife's jointure. The main building on the estate was a dilapidated castle which dated back to medieval times.

The village of Ardglass, which had once been a centre of the herring fishing industry and a flourishing port for commerce with Britain - the old warehouses on the quays still exist - had fallen into decay. In 1741 it was described as being in a 'mean condition consisting of a few ordinary cabins and four or five decayed castles'. At the turn of the century its population was said to be only about 150 people. To mark its connection with the Fitzgeralds there was a street named 'Kildare Street. In later years to commemorate the Beauclerks there was a hotel named 'St. Albans'.

It is not clear as why Ogilvie should have bought this property - he was said to be hostile towards Ireland, and his wife was still alive and living in London -but he may have regarded it as a bargain, and no doubt wanted some substantial asset to bequeath to his daughters. In any event he soon set about reconstructing the village as well as his own house, and restoring the potential of the lands, 'in a whirlwind of reforming enthusiasm' according to his agent, John Wilson. He had always had a feeling for the various grand houses where he had lived - Carton, Leinster, Black Rock, Aubigny, La Verrerie, and Grosvenor Place - but now for the first time he had his own money and was completely in charge. He was a natural entrepreneur, and had his mind set on building a larger harbour and re-opening trade with Britain. In a document dated September, 1808 he submitted plans to the viceroy which envisaged a new pier which would shelter bigger boats. He also got an architect to prepare plans to rebuilt the local anglican church of St. Nicholas for which he eventually subscribed £1,100. To show his ecumenical spirit he gave free land for a Roman Catholic church. In 1813 the Irish parliament gave permission for the proposed longer pier, and the famous engineer Sir John Rennie was employed to supervise the work.

Ogilvie's ambitions for the new harbour are set out in the following letter: 'The proposal for so many works, as well as the number of people who come in summer to Ardglass to take a package to the Isle of Man, have induced me to determine on building a commodious hotel. I also intend to establish a package boat between Ardglass and Port Peel ... As a baker and a brewer will likewise be wanted I have desired Mr. Wilson to inquire for a man who would undertake both, from Scotland. The prices of lime are so high and supplies so uncertain that I have decided to build a lime-kiln; and I desire you to ask Captain Blair if he is decided on setting up salt-pans and what capital he can engage us, if he does not, I will engage another person'. Ogilvie then went on to encourage the local manufacture of linen as he felt that small tenant farmers could not pay their rents unless they had a second source of income. As he grew older he naturally became slower in his ways, and he always regretted that he did not achieve more in re-building Ardglass. In a poignant letter he wrote when he was very old he said of his efforts: 'I am sorry that I undertook it at so late a period of life; it distresses me in every way. I wed a beautiful Duchess, the noble daughter of a Duke, but I have failed to tame the waves on the beach at Ardglass'.

Ogilvie's frustrations about building a pier were softened by his happy relations with Emily and several of his grandchildren. The old rows which had scarred their earlier years were now forgotten. They wrote each other long letters across the Irish Sea, and occasionally members of the family came to Co. Down. In 1830 one of his grand-daughters wrote that 'Papa', as they called him, was still busy 'making pence'. In the autumn of that year Emily (then aged 52) wrote a long letter to her daughter Katherine saying how happy she was, along with her son Aubrey William, to be staying at Ardglass. 'The weather here is delicious. I never saw anything so beautiful as the sea opposite to me at this moment, rippling in and sparkling with sunshine among the rocks and small bays that surround this house'. It was a cheerful note to end on what was probably her last visit to see her father. Two years later exactly (on 18th November, 1832) old Ogilvie was dead. He left the estate to Aubrey William who had a plaque put up in St. Nicholas'. It read:

Sacred to the memory of William Ogilvie, Esq. of Ardglass Castle, who departed this life on the 18th November, 1832, in the 92nd year of his age and was here interred. In the year 1774 he married Emily Lennox, Dowager Duchess of Leinster, and by her had two daughters Cecelia, wife of C. Lock Esq, of Norbury Park, Surrey, and Emily, wife of C.G. Beauclerk, Esq. of St. Leonards Forest, Sussex. A long life and a powerful constitution, unimpaired by the vices of society, which he devoted to useful purposes, enabled him to restore the ancient tower of Ardglass which had fallen into ruin. He erected this church, established a school, and constructed the harbour - works which will long remain testimonies of his energy, industry, and attachment to his tenantry. The unswerving consistency and regularity of his habits caused him to pass through life afflicted by few infirmities. He retained the vigour of his mind to the last, and dying, regretted by a numerous family, left behind him an example worthy of the imitation of every landlord in Ireland.

IN THE WAKE OF CAPTAIN COOK:
THE TRAVELS OF GORDON AUGUSTUS THOMSON (1799-1886),
principal donor of Ethnographic objects to the Ulster Museum, Belfast

by Winifred Glover

The Ethnographic collection in the Ulster Museum, Belfast contains approximately 4,000 specimens. Although relatively small numerically, it contains some important early specimens and most of these come from the collection of Gordon Augustus Thomson, an Ulsterman whose travels took him to many parts of the world which Cook's voyages made accessible for the first time. The eighteenth century was remarkable for the progress made in expanding man's knowledge of the world. The three epic voyages of Captain James Cook from 1769-1776, following on earlier voyages of discovery by Dutch, Portuguese and French explorers, opened up the Islands of the Pacific Ocean to the not always benign benefits and advantages of the 'civilised' world.

At the very end of this remarkable century, on 21 September 1799 at Whitehouse on the old family estate of Castleton or Jennymount, was born Gordon Augustus Thomson, a man extraordinary for his time and place. He was the third son of John Thomson (1766-1824) one of the original directors of the Belfast Banking Company. His mother was Anne Wilson, a sister of Walter Wilson a shipbuilder. The family, of Scottish descent, was wealthy, well-connected and strongly Presbyterian. Gordon Augustus' great grandfather, John Thomson (1691-1765), was Presbyterian Minister of Carnmoney for 34 years. His grand uncle the Hon Robert Gordon had settled in the island of St Vincent in the West Indies as Governor. His nephew, General Sir E. Selby Smith, was one of the commissioners of the Colonial and Indian Exhibition in London in 1851.

From this highly conventional family came Gordon Augustus, possibly the least conventional Ulster Presbyterian ever born. In later life he never practised any profession, but roamed the world for years, accompanied by a foreign servant; although privileged to mix in the highest society he still sought the company of convicts and the excitement of minor cloak-and-dagger diplomacy. Many of the events in his life were remarkable but they are, however, hard to put in order since all his biographers agree that he never wrote anything down. The only written account of his travels was dictated to the *Australasian* and published 24 October 1874 entitled 'Early Australian Reminiscences'. This was twelve years before his death when the memory of

46

what had happened some thirty years earlier may have been somewhat confused.

The ostensible reason for his lack of a career and the start of his wanderlust was that he had been sickly as a child. Two sources agree on this fact: his obituary in *The Argus* of 8 June 1886 - 'In early life he was not robust; hence his studies were not closely followed' - and in an account written by his nephew General E. Selby Smith - 'and being delicate in his youth he was kept at home by my grandfather and never given any professional calling'.

His parents died in 1824, his father on 6 May and his mother on 7 November. In either 1826 or 1828 he accepted an offer from his grand uncle to live in the kinder climate of the West Indies and so he sailed for St Vincent on board a sugar brig, the only means of direct travel in those days. His grand uncle's plantation was called Bedeque, a name Thomson was fondly to re-use several times in the future for the houses which he built. It was here that he collected his first foreign object, a stone axe head now in the Ulster Museum.

Another reason for his departure is said to have been that Thomson had contracted an unfortunate marriage in 1824 from which two female children were born, Mattie and Margaret. These children were adopted by two different families. The story was told by the late Miss Mary Scott Rooney (personal communication), herself the great-granddaughter of the elder girl. Thomson was then shipped off by his family and more or less paid to stay away. In later life he never had money worries and throughout all his travelling he never carried money with him, relying on letters of credit from his agents Richard Jones and Co. of Sydney and Kemp and Co. of Hobart, Tasmania.[1] His brother John, Head Director of the Belfast Banking Company, was instrumental in ensuring that Gordon Augustus got money.

It is difficult to place credence on the sickly childhood theory since, throughout his life, he was a great horseman and lived to the great old age of eighty-seven, after a lifetime of arduous travel on whaling ships and any other ship available, not to mention marathon horseback rides lasting many days over the Pampas of South America. His portrait painted in his eighty-sixth year depicts a healthy looking, serene old gentleman from whom the devils of his youth had passed. (Plate 1) The passport or travel document which he held during his journeying throughout Middle and South America from 27 February 1841 until 3 April 1843 describes him as 42 years of age, unmarried, with blonde hair and blue eyes, an ordinary nose, a large mouth, a full beard and of tall stature. It also mentions, on the occasion of his going to Mexico in 1843, that he carried arms for his defence.

Miss Rooney said that his nickname was 'Galloper' because he was reputed to have ridden from Belfast to Dublin for a wager. Later research reveals that this had been a common misconception, for 'Galloper' Thomson and Gordon Augustus Thomson were not the same person. 'Galloper' Thomson, whose appealing and youthful portrait hangs in the Linenhall Library, Belfast, was the cousin of Gordon Augustus. His portrait shows a confident young man with brown eyes and auburn hair whereas Gordon Augustus clearly had blue eyes and blond hair. 'Galloper' died young after a life of debauch and excess and it is most likely he who fathered the two small girls[2]. In any event, Gordon Augustus' subsequent career indicates that women figured low among his interests.

In 1831 his uncle Colonel Gordon died, having named Gordon Augustus as his heir. Shortly after this he was invited by Captain Richard Meredith of H.M.S. *Pelorus* to join him for a 'cruise' in African waters. This cruise took the form of hunting slave ships and, while he was on board, a large slaver carrying 460 negroes was captured. Thomson was revolted by the conditions on board[3]. This adventure took place off Sierra Leone and the *Pelorus* sailed for Benin, again in quest of slavers. On this occasion Thomson told his nephew that one dark night the ship almost came into conflict with another British man-of-war, both vessels believing the other was their quarry, a notorious slaver. The *Pelorus* appears then to have called at Cape Town where Thomson disembarked and spent six months exploring the African continent. In the years 1831-37, the *Pelorus* sailed up the east coast of Africa to Madagascar, Mozambique and the Indian Ocean as far as Ceylon, but whether he again travelled on board this ship has not yet been established.

In June 1834, Thomson is listed as giving a collection of African objects to the Belfast Natural History & Philosophical Society. They are as follows: Models of a Bushman and Woman, made by the Moors in Africa; an Amopondes Battle-Axe, Snuff-box, and Knife; a Caffer's Spear, Fowling Club, Snuff-box and Pipe; Two drinking Baskets; Specimens of the Language of some of the African tribes, printed by English Missionaries in Africa; a large Carross or Blanket, made of Leopards' Skins, used by the Native Kings: a Zooler's Battle-Axe: Two Specimens from the cango Grotto: a Skin of a Young Ostrich; Five Ostrich's Eggs: a Nest of the Woolbird, or Cape Titmouse: a

Nest of the Bushfinch or Hanging Grosbeak: Minerals from the Bed of the Great Orange or Gariep River: Eyes of the Black Whale: a Foulah's Sword and Bow: a Quiver and Poisoned Arrows: Case of Eye Powder: Extracts from the Koran: a Mandingo's Knife, Snuff-box and Spoon: Fetish or Charm: a Foulah's Sword and Hat: a Tusk of a Sea-Cow: a Young Porpoise: a Shark's Jaws: a Porcupine Fish: Lava and shells from the Island of Ascension: Magnetic Stone from Sierra Leone: Three Land Tortoises: Two Poisoned Arrows, etc. etc. from the Cape of Good Hope. The specimens of the language of South African tribes printed by English missionaries are dated 1832 so he must have been in Africa until at least the beginning of that year. He must also have shipped the objects back to Ulster because, according to his nephew Selby Smith, he did not return to Ulster until 1843.

From Africa he set sail for the island of St Helena where he stayed a short time. Much later in life, on 17 April 1878, he was to write to the Trustees of the Public Library in Melbourne offering them a case containing Napoleon's hair. Since Napoleon had died on St Helena in 1821, Thomson was obviously opportunist in acquiring the relic on his way to Bombay in 1833. From St. Helena he set sail for India, Singapore, China and Japan about 1833 or 1834. It was in Bombay that he purchased the chart of the route to the Red Sea now in the Ulster Museum.

Throughout his life Thomson was able to call on letters of introduction from many wealthy and titled people which enabled him to gain easy acceptance into many communities where Europeans were newly establishing themselves. When he arrived in Bombay he was introduced to Lord Clare who furnished him with letters of introduction to the government officials and 'native potentates' east of Bombay[4]. It would seem from the objects that Thomson collected that he went from Bombay, round the Bay of Bengal to Madras, then Calcutta then via Malaya to Canton and Manilla in the Philippines. On 22 July 1834, he was given a passport from Coorg Ragah by Lieutenant Kerr. This passport took the form of a pellet of hardened clay impressed with a character of three-quarter inch diameter. On 3 March 1833 he purchased two paintings by an Indian artist of the Indian gods Narasimha and Ganesha at Jaipur.

Although he spent almost nine months in India he made a collection of only 29 objects, but since one of these was a set of arrows and a bow and another a flintlock rifle, he may have spent some of his time hunting with the native potentates mentioned by

Humphreys (1882, 177). He then apparently returned a second time to China where in Canton he was the guest of Thomas Dent, a wealthy Hong Kong merchant. Some time during the year 1835 he embarked on *The Lady of the Lake*, Captain Pearson commanding, for Sydney. On his journey the ship apparently called at the Philippine Islands where, 10 October 1835, he purchased a piece of cloth and a couple of shirts in Luzon.

According to Humphreys (1882) he had a short stay in Sydney then crossed to Tasmania. There, in June 1836, he travelled overland from Hobart Town to Launceston. Taking a small boat from there on the river Tamar, manned by two ticket-of-leave men as rowers, he made for George Town. Even this short journey was eventful for, losing their way in the fog and dark of approaching night, they met a boat with a single oarsman who hailed them and directed them to a hut where they could spend the night. During the 3 or 4 days which Thomson spent in George Town he learned that their Good Samaritan was a notorious bushranger with a large bounty on his head. Thomson says, 'He was, I believe, afterwards hanged, but I do not at the moment remember his name', rather a sad epitaph.

His next venture was to cross the Bass Straits from Tasmania to Port Phillip, now Melbourne, in a schooner filled with crates of sheep. In the 1830s it had become obvious to the settlers in Tasmania that the expansion in New South Wales offered much greater possibilities for sheep farming. On arriving at Port Philllip, Thomson made his way to Batman's Hill where John Batman, a former Tasmanian resident who had travelled to the mainland on behalf of the Port Phillip Association, resided in a dwelling which not only had a chimney but also a boarded floor. Since the other huts were made of wattle and daub it indicates the eminence of Batman's position. The members of the Port Phillip Association had acquired a concession of 600,000 acres from the Aborigines around Port Phillip[5].

It was in Port Phillip (Melbourne) that Thomson contracted a curious friendship. Living in one of the huts was William Buckley, 'the wild white man', who for the trifling offence of stealing a piece of cloth (a crime of which he was innocent, he always claimed) had been cashiered from his Cheshire Infantry Regiment and sent to a penal colony. He escaped with two companions in 1803 and for the next thirty years he lived with the Aborigines of Victoria, taking two native wives. At the time of his meeting with Thomson, Buckley had only just received a pardon from Governor Arthur (dated 25 August

1835). When he returned to European life he was widely despised by the European settlers who described him as 'a most repulsive looking rascal 6ft 5$^1/_2$ ins in height', 'he was a man of no intelligence and during his long sojourn with the Blacks had not taught them anything but had settled down into their barbarous ways'[6]. In fairness to Buckley, in an account which he later dictated to John Morgan[7], he emerges as a man of some sensibilities with a genuine fondness for the native groups among whom he had lived and he was certainly a man of sound intelligence and courage, though not necessarily good sense. He does not, however, mention Thomson in his life story.

Thomson says the reason for their friendship was that he had carried an invitation to Buckley from a Tasmanian hotelkeeper in Launceston who had been a fellow prisoner with Buckley, to come over to Launceston and enjoy his hospitality free of charge for the rest of his life. From this 'and other causes combined', Thomson and Buckley formed a friendship and often went hunting together in the bush. When Thomson finally took his leave, Buckley gave him the native axe which he had owned during most of his thirty years among the Aborigines. Thomson donated this axe to the National Museum of Victoria in 1874 where it remains. (NMV Reg. No.X1519). Thomson drew a map of the new settlement at Port Phillip and when he later visited Sydney, staying in Bridge Street in the house of an engraver named Flint, he gave permission for it to be published. Thomson had no desire to 'go into speculation' and allowed Flint to publish it in exchange for copies of the map to give to friends.

Thomson stayed about a month in Melbourne returning to Launceston in the *Vansittart* in July 1836. In Launceston he received and accepted an invitation for 16 July 1836 to a ball and supper given by Major Fairweather and the officers of the 21st Fusiliers to His Excellency Sir George Arthur on the occasion of his departure with his family to England. This was not an event to which his friend William Buckley would have been invited. The following month he set off for Sydney in *The Lady of the Lake*, under the command of Captain Pearson. During his stay in Sydney he became a Corresponding Member of the Belfast Natural History and Philosophical Society. Also at this time he was invited to accompany William Marsden, the notoriously vicious New South Wales missionary[8], to New Zealand as a schoolmaster, the Maoris having asked Marsden to obtain one for them from the King of England. Thomson declined the honour and whether or not he actually visited New Zealand, he collected two New

Zealand *taniko* cloaks and a jade ear ornament.

Thomson's Pacific voyaging seems to have given him the impetus to be a serious collector and actively to follow the routes taken by previous explorers. We know for certain that he visited Tahiti twice, in 1837 and in 1840, and the Hawaiian Islands twice in the year 1840. He may also have visited the Marquesas, Easter, Fijian, Tongan, the Australs and Samoan Islands since he gave objects from all of them. The problem is that though we know he travelled by whaling ship, we do not know in which one, so it has not been possible to check the ships' logs. Another problem is that sailors often collected souvenirs from islands they visited and exchanged them with each other on board ship or sold them to interested buyers. Yet another problem was that Kanakas, who were natives from the Pacific Islands recruited from the island populations, often brought objects with them to trade with the sailors; this may have been the source of some of his collection. This is probably the case with the seven Fijian clubs since the Fijian Islands were one of the last Polynesian groups to be visited and settled by Europeans and it was not until 1860 that permanent settlements were established by European cotton planers and traders. It does however seem certain that he met the 'Queen' of the Marquesas since he says that she gave him a plaited pandanus fan with a carved wooden handle. There was in fact no overall Queen of the Marquesas at this time but there is a possibility he met a high chieftainess and it is further possible that the amazing leg reproduced in Plate 2 belonged to her: it bears the tattoo of a Marquesan lady of rank called Queen Tahiatanani. If this was the leg, what must the whole woman have been like!

The Pacific Islands which Thomson visited existed in an altered state in the aftermath of the great Cook explorations. Of the Marquesas Islands Cook had written in 1774: 'The inhabitants of these Islands are without exceptions as fine a race of people as any in this sea or perhaps any whatever'. Some sixty years later, in 1834, the French explorer Rear Admiral Du Petit-Thouars described the natives of Fatu Hiva, one of the Marquesas Islands as follows: 'they are no longer savages, they have lost all the originality of their primitive character and as yet all they have acquired from civilisation is its vices'. The problem was that, although Cook was a humane and kindly man, his scientific explorations opened up the Pacific to droves of missionaries, whalers and adventurers of every kind out to exploit a rich new field, spiritual or otherwise.

Portrait of Gordon Augustus Thomson painted by the Australian artist Flintoff in 1885.

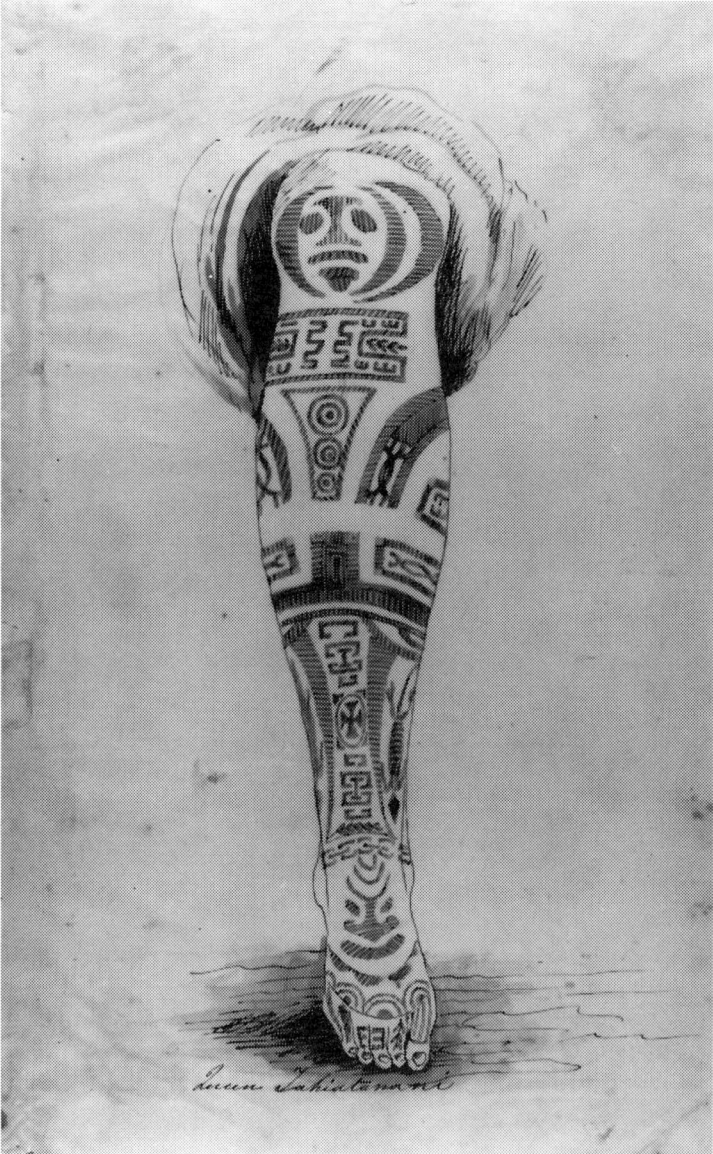

Queen Tahiatanani's leg

Thomson was very much aware of the activities of previous explorers. In Hawaii he collected copies of a list of the articles of arrangements between Thomas H.P. Catesby Jones, Agent of the United States for Commerce and Seamen, and Kaukeaouli, King of the Sandwich Islands and his guardians, Oahu 23 December 1826, reprinted in 1836; a copy of the Treaty between Great Britain and the Sandwich Islands between Kamehameha III and Captain Edward Russell of His Britannic Majesty's Ship *Acteon*, printed November 1836 and a letter from Captain George Vancouver to the King of Hawaii on 2 March 1794. He also collected a mirror which had been left by Captain Vancouver in Hawaii in 1796. Vancouver had been one of the officers on Cook's third and final voyage, so Thomson was well aware of the explorations which had already been undertaken.

Thomson twice met Pomare IV, Queen of the Society Islands (1813-77), and from her letter written to him on 23 January 1840 it is obvious that they had exchanged presents. The fine tapa cloth in the royal colour yellow, imprinted with a red leaf design, is probably one of her gifts to him. Thomson, however, does not mention her in any of his reminiscences, even though at the time of their meeting she was young and attractive. nor does he mention Queen Tahiatanani who was, if anything, even more memorable. He bought from Princess Boki, one of the Hawaiian Royal Princesses, the ermine cloak which King George IV had sent to the Queen of Hawaii. He was given a piece of tapa cloth by Kapiolani, an important Hawaiian chieftainess, yet he never mentions or describes her. From Elisabeta Kinau, who was the daughter of the famous King Kamehameha I who had united all the Hawaiian Islands under his power, he purchased a ring and ball game of which the ball was a little gourd nose flute with the name 'Kinau' burned on to the surface, yet he never refers to his meeting with her even though she was at the height of her fame when they met.

In his reminiscences for the *Australasian*, when talking of Melbourne, he says 'I cannot from recollection say anything about the female population although, of course, some of the settlers had their families with them.' His obituary in the *Argus* mentions that 'Mr Thomson never married and he retained to the end of his days "bachelor habits"'. General Selby Smith wrote: 'Mr Gordon Thomson never married. He was fond of having favourite men servants during his erratic career and afterwards when settled at home. He always provided for them by enabling them to be placed in good occupations.' The truth seems to have been that Thomson had little interest in women and it may have been that his regard for his men servants was more than polite society could accommodate. This would have been a potent reason for his hasty departure from Ireland and for staying away for seventeen years, funded by money from his family. It would also explain his reluctance to write down a detailed account of his travels since it is easier to remain secret if one has committed nothing to paper.

On 27 February 1838, he was in Rio de Janeiro with a letter of safe conduct from the resident Consul Robert Hesketh. Thomson volunteered to carry dispatches of importance from Rear Admiral Charles B. Ross who commanded H.M. naval forces in the Pacific. He also carried dispatches on horseback through the Pampas and later revelled in recounting his escapes from Pampas robbers. Thomson travelled through Chile, Peru and eventually to Mexico where he formed an acquaintance that was to have a profound effect on his life. Santiago Pedro Castenon was engaged as his new native servant and was to accompany him on his travels until the year 1843 when Thomson returned to Ireland.

On 20 April 1839 he set sail for Hönolulu on the *Clementine* bound for Sitka and California. The ship was commanded by Captain Handly. On this voyage he described himself as a naturalist in search of specimens and is named on the passenger list as George A. Thomson called also Gordon H. Thomson.[9] He carried letters of introduction from John C. Jones to the Governor of California and General Vallejo.[10] For company there was on board, Captain John A. Sutter[11], two German cabinet makers and nine kanakas (Sandwich Island Gazette, 27 April 1839).

When visiting the Hawaiian Islands he again carried a letter of introduction from John Adams Kuakini, an influential governor of Hawaii and half-brother of the famous dowager Queen Kaahumanu. In this letter he is described as a surveyor: evidently Thomson liked to appear in different guises. It also demonstrates with what ease he could obtain letters of introduction from whatever influential person he needed. Thomson enjoyed his sojourn in the Hawaiian Islands. On 12 September 1839 he was sent a letter from King Kamehameha III enclosing three little bunches of red and yellow feathers used in making the royal feather cloaks. The text makes sad reading, emphasising the monumental changes which had taken place in Hawaiian society since the Islands were first discovered by Captain

Cook on 18 January 1778. Kamehameha writes: 'when you look at these you will perhaps call to mind what Hawaii was'. (Letter in Ulster Museum collection).

From California he went up the coast to Sitka in Alaska where he stayed for several weeks in May 1839. There he collected some Aleutian Eskimo specimens, including six pieces of sealskin money used by the Russians in trading with the Aleuts and a fine painted wooden helmet. On 1 July 1839 he returned to San Francisco and on 10 August the *Sandwich Island Mirror* relates that he again set sail on the *Clementine* with Captain Handly for Honolulu. It would appear that he remained in Honolulu from August 1839 until January 1840 when he again visited Tahiti. It was also in 1840 that he became an Honorary Member of the B.N.H.& P.S.

On 27 February 1841, he set off with Santiago for a long tour through South America. Santiago also accompanied him to the United States, Upper and Lower Canada from Niagara to Thomson's estate called Bedeque in Prince Edward Island. From New Orleans they travelled to Vera Cruz, then Mexico city then by English steamer the *Thames* to Havana and New Orleans. Thomson was bringing Santiago back home with him when the servant died suddenly in Liverpool. Devastated, Thomson suffered what amounted to a nervous breakdown. In the midst of his grief he was comforted by a Wesleyan minister and, from that day until his death, Thomson adhered to Wesleyan Methodism[12]. From that time on also he became a religious and philanthropic man. On his return to Belfast in 1843, as a memorial he donated Santiago Pedro Castenon's small collection of Mexican artefacts to the Belfast Natural History & Philosophical Society as well as his own much larger collection.

His good works included visiting the sick in the Belfast Royal Hospital, paying £3 for a grave for Margaret Claire Close, possibly a servant or perhaps just a destitute patient. He became a Member of Belfast Town Council for Dock Ward on 25 November 1849 and continued as a councillor until he resigned in 1854. At this time his address was 109 Donegall Street. He served on several sub-committees such as the Property Committee, the General Purposes Committee, the Audit Committee, the Custom House Committee, the Committee on Police Affairs and the Appeal Committee. According to the Minute Book he was an assiduous attender at all meetings for the first two years, but during the final years he was absent from quite a few.

He also continued as a member of the B.N.H.& P.S., contributing observations on his travels at many of the meetings. The *Proceedings* of the B.N.H.& P.S. for 21 January 1857 relate that, after a paper on volcanoes had been read, Thomson regaled the assembled members with his reminiscences about climbing Mauna Loa, the giant volcano on the island of Hawaii which is active to this day. In the *Proceedings* for 22 April 1857, after a lecture on the whale, he again related his adventures on board a whaling ship in the Pacific. It is hardly surprising that he found council meetings on the public nuisance of the Blackstaff River flooding houses in Sandy Row tame by comparison.

At first he resided with his brother Robert at Jennymount although he appears to have lived at the address in Donegall Street too. In 1851 he built a house called Bedeque House on the Crumlin Road where the Mater Hospital now stands. Although the house is now gone, Bedeque Street still remains, at least in part. A charming painting of Bedeque House as it was, by the artist Frank McKelvey, is in the Ulster Museum's collection.

In 1866 or -67 he set out again but this time his travels took him for a tour of the Holy Land. Here again, according to his obituary, influential introductions gave him large opportunities for observation.

Although he was apparently offered opportunities in civil and religious spheres, Thomson remained the essential outsider. In 1872 he set sail for Melbourne where he continued as a decidedly religious man in a house which he again called Bedeque in Dudley Street. His friends included the Rev. A. M. Henderson, the minister of Collins Street Independent Church and Sir Arthur Kennedy, Governor of Queensland.[13]

Perhaps the final word should be left to his nephew General Selby Smyth. 'His life during all those long years of travel I am afraid was rather purposeless for from all that he had seen and gone through in days when travelling was more difficult and dangerous in foreign lands and seas than it is now. And he would never allow any of his travels to be placed in the hands of a publisher and so everything is lost beyind the few anecdotes which probably few others remember except myself. And yet a most enjoyable book might have been compiled and offers were made to do so.'

Although Thomson obviously enjoyed his travels to Australia and the Hawaiian Islands in particular and, although he collected many fine objects with a connoisseur's eye, it is difficult to gauge his attitude to the native populations he encountered. He did call the

Australian Aborigines 'blacks' but then so did everybody else at that date. When he was in the Hawaiian Islands he desecrated several graves bringing back two skulls and several leg bones. A short account in the Ulster Museum's files reads as follows: 'Bodies found in sitting posture the palms of the hands placed under the thighs. In consequence of the plunder committed by Europeans the cemeteries (unreadable portion) have been buried. They are situated in lava caves and from the nature of the soil and climate the bodies become mummified. (Mr Thomson removed these heads from the trunks himself). No artificial means of altering the shape of the head is practised in the Sandwich Islands and both heads were taken from the same cemetery. Heads elevated like the most elevated of these are frequent among the inhabitants'. The reason Thomson was interested in the shape of the heads was because he had been on the Northwest Coast of America where deforming the head by pressing the fronts of the skulls of newborn babies was the custom. The sloping forehead produced was meant to be a mark of the highborn. This interested Thomson so much that he brought home one of the cedar wood cradles used by the mothers for that purpose. In all Thomson's extensive wanderings round the globe he collected only 344 specimens, a modest number in comparison with other collectors in the Ethnographic field. Their importance lies in the fact that they were collected at a time when the native peoples he visited were still making artefacts using traditional methods and traditional materials, even though their entire lifestyles were undergoing massive and irreversible change.

When he died at his Dudley Street home on 7 June 1886 he left his remaining property and money to his last servant (although as Selby Smyth says by that time he had little left). The servant subsequently was employed in one of the grandest houses of Melbourne. His monument in Balmoral or Kew Cemetery in Melbourne is a fine one but it does not quite fit in with its surroundings. It is in the form of an obelisk soaring to the sky, in stark contrast to the ornate Victorian grave slabs by its side. His finest memorial remains the 344 native objects he collected from his Pacific voyaging in the wake of Captain Cook.[14]

NOTES

1. Thomson, G. A., Early Australian Reminiscences, *Argus*, October 24, 1874, Melbourne
2. So bad was 'Galloper's' reputation that on his deathbed he was heard to say that he 'would rather have his horse and Jennymount than the highest seat in Heaven'. When he was dying a young female cousin leaned near so that he could bestow a final kiss. She sprang back with a scream, her face seared where his lips had touched. He died unrepentant with the name of his beloved Jennymount on his lips. From the time of his death a ghostly horseman galloped the roads round Whitehouse and Jennymount Mill for many years, according to popular legend. *Belfast Newsletter* 8 February 1836
3. Humphreys, H. M. *Men of the Time in Australia,* Melbourne, 1882, pp 177-8
4. Ibid. p.177
5. Burroughs, P. *Britain and Australia 1831-1855,* Oxford 1867, p.162
6. 'von Stieglitz, R. Wm. *Diary of Robt. William von Stieglitz* written at Drummondoney 1875 and 1876. Public Record Office of Northern Ireland, T. 1937
7. Morgan, J. *The Life and Adventures of William Buckley,* first published Hobart, Tasmania in 1852 (reprint Caliban books, Sussex 1979)
8. Hughes, R. *The Fatal Shore,* Pan Books, London 1988 pp.187-191
9. Bancroft, H. H. *History of California* Vol. V, 1848 p.747
10. General Mariano G. Vallejo in 1850 offered land for the new state capital of California. His offer was accepted.
11. Captain John Augustus Sutter was a German-born pioneer settler and colonizer in California. He reached California in 1839 and persuaded the Mexican governor to grant him lands on the Sacramento River. The discovery of gold on his land in 1848 precipitated the California Gold Rush. Ironically this discovery brought him economic ruin for squatters and gold diggers overan his lands, stealing and destroying goods and livstock. Sutter must have just recently arrived in California when he made Thomson's acquaintance on board the *Clementine* on the voyage from California and Sitka. *Encyclopoedia Britannica*, 1988
12. Col. E. Selby Smyth, nephew of G. A. Thomson, letter dated 1892 in private possession and shown to author.

13. *Argus* Tuesday 8th June 1886, p. 6, Thomson's Obituary
14. *The Land of the Brave,* contains Thomson's North American
    Indian collection in the Ulster Museum (Blackstaff Press 1978).
    Polynesia illustrates the Polynesian part of Thomson's collection.
    (Ulster Museum publication No. 1 255, 1987)

HORSEMAN, PASS BY: IRISH-AUSTRALIAN
GRAVESTONES

by Dr Trevor McClaughlin

Today, Australia deals with death like most other western countries, in a deodorized and distant manner. Perhaps the tragic images from Ethiopia and Somalia which have appeared on our television screens have helped de-sensitize us and prevent us from making any deep public display of our grief. Occasionally, we trespass upon the private grief of individuals by reading death notices in newspapers or about the funerals of the rich and famous. In private, of course, things are very different and, in practice, Australia has a rich variety of ethnic groups each of which celebrate death in their own distinctive fashion. But superficially and in the main we seem to be heading in the direction of an American way of death as represented by their funeral parlour slogan, 'You die and we do the rest'.[1]

Such a state of affairs has not always been the case. There is indeed scope for a study of changing Australian attitudes to death, over time, from the Dreamtime to the present. Merely talking to some of the elderly members of our community brings to light some of the changes which have occurred in the last forty or fifty years. Old folks lament that the slow funeral procession, the black crepe billowing in the breeze, the 'outwalkers' flanking the hearse, is a thing of the past. The cortege now speeds by on its way to the cemetery or crematorium, unwilling to hold up the traffic. No one stops to remove their hat or pay their respects. Visits to the cemetery are no longer a frequent occurrence made at some discomfort to the mourner. At best they happen two or three times a year, on Mother's Day or Father's Day and at Christmas.

However impressionistic all this is it is nonetheless a useful starting point. Recollections such as these, oral history in other words, will be an important source in any study of Australian attitudes to death over time. The interested student will also want to consult G. M. Griffin and D. Tobin, *In the Midst of Life ... The Australian Response to Death*, Melbourne University Press, 1982, probably the first book of its kind in Australia. From the vantage point of its authors, one an Uniting Minister the other a funeral director, it provides a fascinating survey of European burial practices and mourning customs. The subject obviously has wide appeal and should attract interest and discussion in academic and other circles in the years to come.

This essay, however, has more modest aims. It merely wants to pass on to the reader some of the author's impressions of changing Irish-Australian attitudes to death and to inform acolyte family historians of the very precise information sometimes contained on Australian headstones. It was sparked off by a report, in a Sydney newspaper, of a woman who had been mugged. Having had her handbag snatched, she appealed for its return: it contained the cremated remains of her husband. She had been carrying his remains in her handbag for the past two years, in readiness for the day when she might take them back to Ireland. Assuming the story was not a hoax, here we were in the late twentieth century being confronted by an age-old belief from peasant Ireland that one should be buried in Ireland, a belief held by many an Irish migrant to the Antipodes during the nineteenth century and yet one which could be so rarely acted upon. The questions almost posed themselves: what attitudes and customs relating to death had the Irish brought with them to Australia? Had many, or any, of them survived? Like Irish settlement in Australia generally, which concentrated neither on the frontier nor in urban ghettoes, Irish attitudes to death were gradually and easily assimilated into an Australian way of dying. In the long run, they became noted for their ordinariness rather than being distinctive or aberrant.

Recently, for example, it has become fashionable to describe Ireland as having a funerary culture or as having a preoccupation with death which stretches from the megalithic tombs of New Grange to the politics of the late twentieth century.[2] However accurate this claim may be, little evidence exists for such a preoccupation on the part of the Australian-Irish. Indeed, the laconic, down-to-earth Australian character would eschew such a romanticized adulation of death. Australian circumstances were very different from Irish ones. Loneliness, isolation, the tyranny of distance militated against the development of that kind of culture, the sentimentality of balladeers notwithstanding. Isolation and the vastness of Australia were the very things which the balladeers extolled in their description of 'the dying stockman' or 'the stockman's last bed',

His whip it is silent, his dogs they do mourn
His steed looks in vain for his master's return,
No friend to bemoan him unheeded he dies,
Save Australia's dark sons no one knows where he lies.[3]

How could the old customs and old ways of celebrating death

have survived in such a new and totally different environment? Different political realities, the demands of land and economy, the harshness of the landscape and the urgency of the living stopped Irish Australians from developing a fixation with death. But some survivals there were. The word 'wake' passed into Australian currency although what it signifies nowadays is but a pale shadow of its former Irish self. So, too, many an Irish Australian used gravestones to record and identify where exactly in Ireland they came from. Their headstones display a well developed and acute Irish sense of place.[4]

Fragments of evidence exist to show that the Irish brought their wake customs with them to Australia. In October 1794 Deputy Judge Advocate David Collins recorded in his *Account of the English Colony of New South Wales*, the burial of the murdered Simon Burn

> This poor man was buried by his widow (an Irish woman) in a corner of his own farm, attended by several settlers of that and the neighbouring districts, who celebrated the funeral rites in the manner and with orgies suitable to the disposition and habits of the deceased, the widow and themselves. [5]

Evidently the traditions of peasant Ireland were alive and well in early New South Wales. As in Ireland clerical opposition would in time lead to the disappearance of such 'orgies'. Moreover, the new Australian environment could never offer enough support for traditional peasant Irish culture. What did survive was the meaning of the wake as a mourning, sometimes as a death watch, when friends and relatives sit with the corpse between death and burial, sometimes as an occasion when food and even alcohol (though this is rare) is consumed and the dead is farewelled with tales retold and memories recalled of the dead person's life and the mourner's bond with him or her.[6] Today mourners will 'bring a plate' to a 'wake' but there is no sign of dancing or games or the old peasant customs.

On the other hand, a specific Irish sense of place did survive. This sense of place is particularly evident in Australian cemeteries. Acutely aware of their displacement, of not belonging either to here or there, a number of Irish Australians seem to have striven to preserve their identity in their final resting place. As with others, their gravestone appeals to the passer-by to remember death:

Good people all as you pass by
As you are now so once was I
As I am now you soon will be
Prepare yourselves to follow me

but it also appeals to the passer-by to remember and commemorate a particular individual whose identity merged with and depended upon a precise place of origin: Patrick Bourke, native of Bourisleigh, Co. Tipperary, Ireland, or Winnifred Kennedy native of Wicklow, parish of Hollywood, Ireland. Of the migrants to Australia in the last century, the Irish seem to have felt this need most of all. More than others, they felt the need to carve into their headstone the exact place where they were born, the place they grew up in, 'place' meaning not just a physical place but the people and the memories and the community who identified them. Was the same need felt by Irish migrants in other places? Whatever the reason for the survival of this record of their sense of place, it is a great boon to family historians who today are searching to discover their own roots and to clarify their own identity.

Accompanying this essay are illustrations of this Irish sense of place extracted from my own collection of photographs and graveyard jottings from a variety of cemeteries in Australia. The list takes examples from every county in Ireland and shows how very specific birthplaces were recorded on gravestones. Some examples were easier to find than others. The counties which sent the most migrants to Australia, Tipperary. Cork, Clare, Galway and Fermanagh, for example, were the easiest to find. They were also easiest to find in areas of relatively high Irish settlement, in cemeteries in Telerah and East Maitland in the Hunter Valley in New South Wales, at Kiama, Gerringong and Jamberoo in the Illawarra, south of Sydney where Ulster Irish were to be found in abundance, and at Kilmore, Kyneton and Gordon in Victoria.

In passing, it is worth nothing that many of the earliest burial places for white settlers are lost to us. The majority of those which have survived are general cemeteries with separate sections set aside and marked for different religious denominations, Anglican, Presbyterian, Uniting Church, Roman Catholic, Greek Orthodox, Jews or whatever. They were first established as public cemeteries and administered cemeteries and were as much concerned about public health as anything else. Cemeteries thus tended to be located at least one or two miles from town beyond the rivers or creeks which were the source of a town's water supply. One can only imagine, perhaps

with the help of some of the engravings of S. T. Gill, the funeral
cortege of bullock drays, horses and walkers making their slow way
along a dusty road to the dead person's grave some distance from
town.

Among the more interesting cemeteries is the New Cemetery at
Gordon, just a few miles east of Ballarat, in Victoria. Local historian
and one of the restorers and unofficial caretakers of the cemetery, Roy
Huggins, has told the author that the New Cemetery consists of ten
acres and was allocated when the town was surveyed in 1863-64.
Unfortunately no record exists of the burials made in an earlier
two-acre Pioneer cemetery at the west end of town and no manuscript
record for burials in the New Cemetery before 1878. But what the
New Cemetery has is an impressive collection of Irish Australian
gravestones. The area between Gordon and Ballarat was an intensive
potato farming area and many of the inhabitants of the region are of
Irish descent. Some of these same potato farmers must also have hit
paydirt on the goldfields and been prepared to use it on funeral
monuments. The work at Gordon displays the familiar symbols of
Irishness, celtic cross, shamrock, round tower and harp as well as an
acutely developed Irish sense of place. Performed chiefly by
stonemasons S. Jaegers and sons, F.W. Commons and McDonalds,
and Thorntons, it reaches a standard even higher than that by the same
stonemasons at Ballarat or Melbourne. Gordon is an exceptionally
well preserved, and cared for, example of memorials to the Irish.

Family historians and perhaps schoolchildren in Ireland and
Australia engaged in a joint local history project or the study of
migration and settlememt will be attracted by the very precise
information which such headstones contain. Transcriptions of the
information on headstones in a number of Australian cemeteries have
already been made by enthusiastic genealogists and local historians.
Some have been published or are available in typescript form. May I
suggest that in the first instance interested parties write to the Hon.
Secretaries of major genealogical societies such as, *The Society of
Australian Genealogists, Richmond Villa, 120 Kent St, Sydney 2000,
The Genealogical Society of Victoria, 5th Floor, 252 Swanston St,
Melbourne 3000, The Genealogical Society of Queensland, P.O. Box
423, Woolloongabba, 4102,* or to the *Royal Australian Historical
Society, History House, Macquarie St, Sydney 2000*? They will then be
certain of being guided in the right direction. Perhaps it is not amiss to
suggest that they too may be interested in the other aspects of this

story, an Irish sense of place, the disappearance of funeral customs, and changing attitudes to death, all of which cry out for further research and examination.

NOTES

1. 'Chauna, Lebrun, Vovelle: The New History of Death', E. LeRoy Ladurie, *The Territory of the Historian*, Sussex, 1973, p.275
2. See, for example, N. Witoszek, 'Ireland: A Funerary Culture?', *Studia*, lxxvi, 1987, pp.206-15.
3. 'The Stockman's last bed', Anon., *Old Bush Songs and Rhymes of Colonial Times*, enlarged and revised from the collection of A.B. Patterson, Douglas Stewart and Nancy Keesing eds., Hong Kong, 1981, p.144.
4. On this sense of place, see Patrick Sheerin, 'Genius Faulae: the Irish Sense of Place', *Irish University Review*, xviii no. 2, 1988, pp.191-206; 'The Sense of Place', Seamus Heaney, *Preoccupations. Selected Prose 1968-1978*, London 1980, pp.131-49, and Patrick O'Farrell, 'Defining Place and Home: Are the Irish Prisoners of Place?', *Home or Away? Immigrants in Colonial Australia Visible Immigrants: Three*, David Fitzpatrick ed., ANU, Canberra, 1992, pp.1-18.
5. David Collins, *An Account of the English Colony in New South Wales*, 2 vols., Brian Fletcher ed., Sydney, 1975, I, 328-9; see also Roger Therry on the wake of Abel Death in his *Reminiscences of Thirty Year's Residence in New South Wales and Victoria*, London 1863, Facsimile edition, Sydney, 1974, pp.321-23.
6. In much the same manner as Maurice O'Sullivan described the wake of old Kate Liam in his *Twenty Years A-Growing*, M.L. Davies and G. Thomson trans., New York, 1933.

IRISH-AUSTRALIAN GRAVESTONES

Birthplace   **Burial**

Antrim   Waverley

Erected to the memory of John McAllister late of West Australia Died 10th Feby 1905 aged 63 years RIP Eldest son of the late James McAllister of Tavnachoney Cushendall Co Antrim Ireland

Armagh   Waverley

In loving memory of Rachel Willis born 23rd Sept. 1865 at Derrycorr Co Armagh Ireland Died at Bondi 14th May 1910 Erected by her sister Elizabeth

Belfast   West Geelong

Mary in fond remembrance of her beloved husband James Lyle native of Belfast Ireland who died 6th April 1887 Aged 64 years

Carlow   Bald Hills

Hardy Eustace[1] son of Hardy and Bridget Annie (nee Brown) Eustace of Newtown Co Carlow, died 3 March 1895 aged 52 years

Cavan   Kiama

In memory of Captain O.M. Stevenson VD E Kiama Co. 2nd A.I. Reg. Born Cavan County Cavan Ireland January 25th 1860 died February 11th 1909

Cork   Gordon

Erected by Margaret Burke to the memory of her beloved husband Edmund Burke who departed this life 9th April 1889 Aged 46 years Native of Clenworth County Cork Ireland also his beloved daughter Margaret who died 18th April 1884 aged 3 years, 8 months. May their souls rest in peace Amen Also his wife Margaret died 29th July 1924 aged 78 years

Clare   Yass

In memory of John and Bridget Conroy who departed this life 17th March 1868 aged 65 and 60 years natives of Killaloe Co Clare Ireland Erected by their children

---

[1] *Memorials to the Irish in Queensland*, Daithi UaLorcain ed., Brisbane, 1988 p.45

Clare   Wallan
Erected by her children to the memory of Margaret Moroney Native of
Tulla, Co. Clare, Ireland who died 16th May 1875 aged 66 years RIP

Clare   Ballarat
Erected by John Torpy native of the parish of Kilfenora, Co Clare,
Ireland; in loving remembrance of his beloved wife Bridget died 11th
Jany 1887 aged 54 years, their beloved children John, Michael, James
and Michael Henry who died in infancy. Andrew Died 16th Augt
1890 aged 26 years, Also the above John Torpy died 12th July 1907,
aged 80 years. May their souls rest in peace Amen

Derry   Muswellbrook
Of your charity pray for the repose of the soul of Patrick Rogers of
Kilrea, Co. Derry, Ireland. Who died 31st May 1884 aged 22 years

Donegal   Waverley
In loving memory of Edward Charles son of the late John Loughrey
Binion Clonmany Co Donegal, Ireland and Grand-son of John Hogan
[The Irish Sculptor] who died in the Hospice, Darlinghurst, Sydney
25th July 1911 RIP "To be resigned is to place God between one's
self and suffering" This cross is lovingly erected by his sorrowing
mother, sisters and brothers.

Down   Kiama
In loving memory of Mary Ann Bruce of Knock Co Down Ireland
died 1st August 1905 Aged 64 years Also Alexander Bruce of Knock
Co Down Ireland died 25th January 1920 aged 76 years

Dublin   Field of Mars
Robert beloved husband of Bridget (Delia) Cruikshank born Dublin,
Ireland 1851 Died 29th May 1908 Aged 58 years Sweet Jesus have
mercy on his soul ... Also Delia beloved wife of Robert Cruikshank
born Dublin, Ireland, 1850 Died 15th May 1931

Fermanagh   Bungendore
Dedicated to the memory of Daniel Gallagher (1789-1871) Native of
Ederny County Fermanagh, Ireland Buried Bungendore according to
the rites of the Roman Catholic Church ... Erected by the descendants
of Daniel and Ellen (nee McCaffrey 1809-1860) to commemorate the
150th anniversary of the family's arrival in Australia

Galway   Uralla
Gloria in Excelsis Deo In loving memory of Delia Beloved wife of
Luke Riley who died at Wollun Aug. 17th 1901 Native of Lismakage
Co Galway Ireland Aged 41 years Requiescat in pace Erected to her
memory by her loving husband

Kerry   Sandgate
Thomas Aloysius Bourke Born Tralee Co. Kerry Ireland Nov. 10th
1837 Died at Newcastle, Sept 14th 1907 ... Also Bridget Ethel Bourke
wife of Thomas Aloysius Bourke Born Clashmore, Co. Waterford,
Ireland 17 March 1849, Died Srathfield Sydney 6 Nov. 1929

Kerry   Gundagai
Gloria in Excelsis Deo Sacred to the memory of John J. Quilter A
native of Ballyreehan Co. Kerry Ireland who died at Cobarralong July
29th 1875 aged 78 years Also of his son Thomas William who died at
Cobarralong Dec 25th 1865 aged 10 years On whose souls sweet Jesus
have mercy

Kildare   Telerah
In loving memory of Michael Donnolley Born in Rose Town, Parish
of New Bridge County Kildare, Ireland 29th Sept 1799 Died 28th
August 1875 ...

Kilkenny   Gordon
In loving memory of Thomas Murphy native of Smithstown, Co.
Kilkenny, Ireland Died 29th April 1874 aged 66 years and of his wife
Margaret Died 4th June 1883, aged 86 years. Also of their daughter
Bridget the dearly beloved wife of James Cody died 13th April 1899,
aged 58 years, also the above James Cody Died 31st July 1919, aged
89 years Thomas Cody beloved husband of Ellen Cody Died 26th
April 1918, aged 42 years, RIP

Kings (Laois)   Queanbeyan
Pray for the soul of John Darmody Native of Banagher King's Co
Ireland died at Queanbeyan 20 Feb 1877 Aged 60 years Requieca in
pace Also his beloved wife Mary Darmody who departed this life July
13 1887 Aged 72 years Requiescat in pace

Leitrim   Field of Mars
Mary Ann beloved wife of Francis O'Rourke Native of Ardlougher,
Co. Leitrim died 17th March 1911 aged 57 years RIP

Limerick   Melbourne General
In loving memory of James O'Connell of Richmond who died 21st
July 1904 aged 68 years Native of Shanagolden Co. Limerick Ireland

Limerick   Gore Hill
In loving memory of Patrick Leahy Mayor of Mosman 1905-1909
Born at Foynes Co. Limerick 17th March 1855 Died at Mosman 20th
January 1909 Requiescat

Longford   Waverley
In memory of Anne Farrell Born Longford Eire Died 20th March 1911
Aged 40 years Mary Elizabth Fitzgerald Died 3rd June 1946 RIP

Louth   Field of Mars
In loving memory of our dear son and brother John Joseph McRae
who died in the snow on Mt. Bogong Aug. 1943 aged 27 years Also
Margaret McRae Born Cullon Co. Louth Ireland Died 25th June 1956,
Aged 67 years Also Alexander N. McRae Born Greenock, Scotland
Died 17th Jan. 1972 Aged 86 years RIP

Mayo   Melbourne General
Erected by Ann Joyce to the memory of her beloved husband Thomas
Joyce native of Clarenorris Co Mayo, Ireland who died 15th February
1889 aged 48 years

Meath   Waverley
Sacred to the memory of my dear husband Michael Norris Native of
Kells Co Meath, Ireland who departed this life, 8th May 1910 Aged
57 years ...

Monaghan   Stanthorpe
Charles McKenna b. Truagh Monaghan bur 7 Sep 1911 Stanthorpe

Queen's (Offaly)   Parramatta
Sacred to the memory of John Dunphy late of Queen's County Ireland
who departed this life 23rd April 1856 aged 71 years also Catherine
beloved wife of John Dunphy who departed this life 24th Oct. 1859
aged 55 years May their souls rest in peace Amen

Roscommon   Waverley
Ireland who died 2 December 1891 Aged 46 years

Sligo   Stanthorpe
Ferdinand Trumble McDonagh b. Carrowkeel, Sligo, bur 7 Jul 1933
Stanthorpe

Tipperary   Kyneton

To the memory of Patrick Kelly Native of Kilrowan, Co Tipperary Ireland Died 6th November 1905 age 75 years Also James Kelly Died 8th May 1915 age 79 years Also His beloved wife, Mary Kelly Died 22nd May 1919 age 72 years RIP

Tipperary   Branxton

Of your charity pray for the repost of the soul of Matthew B. Hayes, Native of Pallasmore Co Tipperary Ireland Died 18th June 1904 Aged 70 years

Tipperary   Wangaratta

Michael Cusack 1808-1865 Wangaratta Pioneer Native of Nenagh, Tipperary RIP Erected by his great-grandson L. M. Harris OBE 1981

Tyrone   Queanbeyan

Erected by Francis Devlin to the memory of his beloved wife Catherine native of Anaghmore County Tyrone Ireland who departed this life at Micalgo 1st Nov 1880 in the 65th year of her age Aeternam illi requiem precare viator

Waterford   Waverley

Gloria in Excelsis Deo In loving memory of Patrick O'Brien[2] Native of Strancally Castle County Wexford, Ireland who died 5th July 1898 Aged 83 years

Westmeath   Kilmore

James Allen native of Feakle, County Clare Ireland beloved husband of Theresa Allen who died on 22nd August 1906 aged 75 Also Theresa beloved wife of the above born at Castleost Rochford Bridge Westmeath Ireland 15th April 1838 Died on the 25th of November 1912 Aged 74

Wexford   Kurrajong

In memory of Charles Lary who died August 28 1854 Aged 70 years Charles Lary is my name Ireland is my nation Wexford is my native place And Christ is my salvation Good people all as you pass by As you are now so once was I As I am now you soon will be Prepare yourselves to follow me May he rest in peace Amen

[2] op. cit. p.58

Wicklow   Muswellbrook
Of your charity Pray for the repose of the soul of Winifred Kennedy
Native of Wickow, Parish of Hollywood Ireland Aged 84 years
[broken headstone]

ARCHBISHOP CROLLY AND THE DEVELOPMENT OF CATHOLICISM IN ULSTER 1812-49

by Very Rev. Dr Ambrose MacAuley PP

William Crolly was born at Ballykilbeg near Downpatrick on 8 June 1780.[1] His family, which was of Anglo-Irish origin, had been fairly substantial farmers in that district for many years. William was sent to a nearby school for primary education and thence to a classical school in Downpatrick, which was conducted by the Reverend James Neilson, the Presbyterian minister in the town. Many Irish towns then boasted classical schools; as their name suggests they concentrated on Latin and Greek but also taught English, Mathematics and in some cases French and other subjects, and they prepared their pupils for university education or mercantile careers. Many Presbyterian clergymen conducted such schools in their own manses in the north of Ireland. Dr Neilson's, which was among the best of them, was located not in the manse but in a recognised school-house, and apart from the master usually had at least one assistant. During Crolly's school days this assistant was a Catholic named Doran, who was interned in Downpatrick Jail in 1798 because of his political views. Crolly actually attended classes with him in the prison, and perhaps it was this early encounter with the consequences of nationalist enthusiasm in the uncongenial surroundings of a jail that deterred him in later life from ever showing any enthusiasm for nationalist causes.

In 1801 at the fairly mature age of twenty-one William Crolly enrolled at St Patrick's College, Maynooth. Founded in 1795 as a result of the closure of Irish seminaries in France, that college was still in its teething stages when Crolly joined it. The first set of buildings to house 200 students was completed in 1799. Three of the most prominent professors were exiled French priests and a year after Crolly's enrolment a fourth, Francis Anglade, whom he was destined later to succeed, joined them. Crolly was ordained in 1806 after about four years' study, as illness forced him to spend most of a year at home. Nonetheless he had distinguished himself in his latter years and a month after ordination he was appointed as assistant lecturer in philosophy. Three years later he succeeded Anglade in the chair. His professorial career, however, was destined to be brief.

In 1812 the aged and failing pastor of Derriaghy and Belfast, Hugh O'Donnell, decided to retire, and he and his parishioners sent a deputation to Bishop Patrick MacMullan in Downpatrick to beg him to confer the parish on Crolly. Doubtless the parishioners of Belfast believed that they were offering a suitable field of labour to a scholarly young priest by inviting him to a flourishing town with commercial potential and literary scope. Despite the strong persuasion of Archbishop Troy of Dublin to remain in Maynooth, Crolly accepted the invitation and took up office in Belfast in September 1812.

Belfast had formed part of a united parish with the country district of Derriaghy, but by 1812 it had become much larger than Derriaghy and had a Catholic population approaching 5,000. The parish boundaries, like those of the town, did not cross the Lagan but extended to the north and west several miles, though few Catholics then lived in places like Whiteabbey, Ligoniel and Glengormley. For some years St Mary's had had an active committee of laymen who were elected by the congregation and managed its finances. In 1808 the parish committee obtained a site for a second church from the Marquis of Donegall, and work on this building in Donegall Street was progressing when Crolly arrived. His relations with the committee were not always harmonious. Realising that the congregation was growing fast he decided that a gallery should be added, proposed that the pews in it be sold to those who could afford them, and that the ground floor be left to the poor. But some of the middle class who were rich enough to own pews objected to being consigned to the remoteness of the gallery - perhaps on the biblical principle of not letting their light be hidden under a bushel - and insisted on having their seats on the ground floor. Crolly, however, held out and the prestige of owning a pew ultimately forced the dissidents to capitulate.

The church was eventually blessed and opened under the invocation of St Patrick in 1815. Crolly preached the special sermon on the occasion and expressed particular thanks to his Protestant and dissenting brethren who, through their generous support, had made possible the erection of the church. According to the *Belfast News Letter:*

> He characterised it as the dawn of a brighter day than had yet visited Ireland, when good will and rational ideas of tolerant benevolence should take the place of more inhospitable feelings, and Christians of every religious denomination would henceforth live with each other in harmony and the bond of peace ... He remarked that he had been in different parts of Ireland, but had never seen such benevolence and liberality manifested as in Belfast, where he had now the happiness to reside, and where he hoped to have the honour to spend the remainder of his days. This liberality had done

more than anything that had occurred for a length of time to produce unanimity and cordiality among the people. In fact, it had quite emancipated the Catholics; and if the Protestants throughout Ireland would follow the example, Catholic emancipation would be but a name.

The preacher also disclosed that Protestants had contributed £1,300 and Catholics £2,800 towards the cost of the church, which was upwards of £5,000. The *News Letter* commented that the sermon 'seemed well calculated to gratify every person present, by exhibiting on the one hand generosity and enlightened sentiment, and on the other a grateful and affectionate sense of the protection and favour extended to the Catholics and which cannot fail to have the best effects'.[2]

The Catholic congregation subsequently met to express its thanks to the Protestants of Belfast for their generosity and to Crolly for his 'liberal, enlightened and conciliating discourse - a discourse which must succeed in vindicating the Catholic religion against its calumniators, and in establishing that honest and ingenuous confidence, which all denominations of Christians shall ever repose in its conscientious convictions of one another'.[3] No other church was built in Belfast during Crolly's association with the town, and St Patrick's, popularly known as the New Chapel, in contradistinction to St Mary's, the Old Chapel, was used for all important liturgical and ceremonial occasions.

Taking advantage of the goodwill evidenced by the generosity of Protestants to St Patrick's, Crolly decided that he would hold a series of lectures on the Catholic faith which would be open to all Christians. His purpose was to dispel ignorance and misunderstanding rather than seek converts, and the talks were pitched at the explanatory and ecumenical rather than at the argumentative or polemical level. Attendances were large and appreciative.

On his arrival in Belfast, he had also decided to participate as widely as possible in the general social and literary life of the town; and his urbane and conciliatory manner greatly eased his way into a society that was predominantly Presbyterian. In December 1812 his name was proposed for membership of the Belfast Society for Promoting Knowledge (later known as the Linen Hall Library). In January 1813 he was elected and in the following month was chosen to sit on the governing committee. In the following year he was invited with two other members of the committee to supervise the relocation and cataloguing of the books after they had been displaced because of repairs to the Linen Hall.[4]

He also subscribed to the funds for the erection of the Belfast Academical Institution, which had been launched by the liberals of Belfast and neighbourhood in 1810 to provide tertiary education in arts, theology and medicine, and secondary education both for boys who wished to pursue their studies further or who aspired to a career in business or commerce. Questioned at the commission of inquiry into the Academical Institution in 1825 about the attendance of Catholic boys, Crolly replied that he thought the teachers encouraged them to pay particular attention to their religious and moral duties. While he thought it probable that boys might insult one another about religion on their way to and from school, he felt that there was no cause for complaint about conduct in the Institution. He himself had a student there preparing for the priesthood, and had no objection to other seminarians doing likewise, though he 'might find it, perhaps, desirable to establish a diocesan seminary' and in that case should ... in all probability, give the preference to it.[5]

At the primary level there were two important schools in the town: the Lancasterian school in Frederick Street, founded by Joseph Lancaster in 1811, in which pupils were taught by a male and female teacher with the assistance of monitors or senior students specially selected for that purpose. By 1815 there were seven hundred pupils drawn from all denominations on the rolls, but as attendance was voluntary the numbers present in the classroom varied greatly according to the season of the year, parental interest and state of health. On 8 July 1815 some 300 prizes, consisting of 'bibles, testaments and useful books' for the boys and dresses for the girls were distributed, and Crolly gave the address. Paying tribute to Lancaster for creating such an excellent system of education and to the people of Belfast for founding the schools, which were free and open to all without distinction of means, he called upon the children to appreciate the opportunities they enjoyed. Predicting that the system would produce a most beneficial effect on society, he noted with satisfaction that in the schools

> 'the speculative differences of religious opinion were entirely lost sight of, and Protestant, Presbyterian and Catholic went hand in hand in the benevolent endeavour to be useful' and expressed the hope that 'this liberal and tolerant feeling ... would be still more widely disseminated and [that] Belfast would thereby be improved

and benefitted in an inconceivable degree'.

Warning the children to avoid every kind of unlawful association as not only injurious to society but hostile to their own peace, he concluded by praising Maurice Cross, the headmaster, for his skill and proficiency, and for the order and regularity obtaining in the school.[6]

He continued to support and patronise the Lancasterian school; his relations with the other Belfast school, that of Brown Street, were, however, less happy. That school, founded by more conservative elements in Belfast society, was restored after storm damage in 1816, and by then had 1,000 pupils. Crolly on that occasion was invited by the committee of management to address parents, children and teachers and he continued to attend its meetings regularly. In 1822, however, he was not reappointed to the committee, and his proposal to provide the Catholic children at his own expense with the Douay version of the Scriptures was rejected. Consequently, he withdrew the Catholic children from that school and in 1824 established a Sunday school in St Patrick's Church, which soon had 1,500 pupils on its rolls. The *Northern Whig*, a liberal journal founded in that year, remarked that Crolly's move was 'inspired by the distrust felt by many Catholics for the Sunday School Society and the narrow and ill-advised system of policy adopted by that Institution'.[7]

His participation in other movements to benefit the people of all denominations was more happy. In 1815 he was elected to the board of directors of the newly formed Belfast Savings Bank, which was founded to encourage thrift among the poor. He participated actively in bodies which looked after the social well-being of his fellow townsmen - the House of Industry which provided relief to the unemployed, and the General Hospital, of which he became a manager.

According to the census of 1821 the total population of the town was 37,800. This census was not carried out with the rigorous accuracy that subsequently became common practice and questions about religious affiliation were not asked. Consequently the number of Catholics in the early 1820s is not known. In 1824 a controversy on this subject broke out in the Belfast press between the *Irishman* and the *Belfast News Letter* - the former claiming that the Catholic population could be as high as 13,200 and the latter arguing that it was less than 6,000.[8] Similar arguments broke out over the census of 1834 which put the Catholic population of Shankill, the parish of the established church, as 22,078 out of a total of 67,224. A reasonably safe estimate for the Catholic population of the town in that year would be 21,000. Whatever the true figure in 1824 was, it was higher than that suggested by the *News Letter*.

In that year the Bishop of Down and Connor, Patrick MacMullan, who was aged and infirm, sought permission from Rome for the appointment of a coadjutor. The clergy of the diocese, or most of them, assembled to vote for a candidate of their choice, and the parish priest of Belfast obtained the overwhelming majority of the votes. This decision was popular with the laity of Belfast. John Lawless, the editor of the *Irishman*, paying tribute to Crolly's labours which he said were not more distinguished by zeal than talent, went on to comment on the difficulties facing clergy in proclaiming their own beliefs in such a way as not to offend others of a different persuasion and he concluded:

> As far as we have had an opportunity of observing, the Rev Mr Crolly has greatly succeeded in the execution of this most difficult office. He has satisfied the mind of the Catholic and he has not offended the conscience or the feeling of the Protestant. He has with great address defended his own doctrines without offering the most distant insult to the doctrines of the other men - a rare and valuable merit, and worthy of every minister of the gospel.[9]

Bishop MacMullan died before the appointment could be made. Rome, however, accepted the recommendation of the Down and Connor clergy, supported as it was by the approval of the Archbishops of Armagh and Dublin, and on 6 February 1825 Crolly was formally appointed. He was ordained bishop on 1 May in St Patrick's Church and, on the following evening, 2 May, he entertained to dinner in Ward's Hotel some 250 guests who included the sovereign or mayor, and leading clergy and citizens of all denominations. It was an occasion of warm ecumenical goodwill. The sovereign proposed Crolly's health and in reply the bishop recalled that he had come to Belfast friendless and unknown, but that 'he had not breathed the air of Belfast for many days, when the clergymen of different denominations stepped forward to extend the right hand of fellowship and welcome; nor were the laity slow in following the example'. He rejoiced that his present elevation would afford him more opportunity of proving his gratitude. 'It shall be my constant endeavour', he said, 'to diffuse universal benevolence through the diocese committed to my care; nor shall I cease, while one illiberal member of our church is to be found, from the mountains of Mourne to the caverns of the

Causeway. If there should be any priest tainted by narrow and gross prejudice, I shall send him for his cure to inhale the liberal atmosphere of Belfast'. He was proud to be able to convince Dr Curtis, and his other brethren, that Belfast might well be counted the most liberal and charitable town in any part of Europe. 'Of this there was a standing testimony in the New Chapel, which was built by the generous contribution of every class of Christian - and, I trust', said the worthy prelate, 'that under my care the voice of bigotry has never profaned its walls'... He concluded with hoping that he would never give his townsmen cause to change their favourable opinion of him.

The *Northern Whig* ended its report of the ceremony and celebrations with an enthusiastic description of the genuine concord so evident at the dinner and a palmy forecast of a halcyon, if utopian, future.

> It was not one of those meetings, whose intercourse is confined to the mere pressure of the hand, or the cold exchange of formal civility - it was a meeting of Irish men and of brothers ... It was an anticipation of what may be expected, when Catholic and Protestant are placed upon the same footing and when they learn everywhere to look upon each other - not with the sullen or exasperated glare of party feud but with the kindly beam of brotherly affection. When the apple of discord shall have been forever removed from our island, and faction shall have ceased to embroil its inhabitants, such meetings as this will be no longer contemplated with surprise, and the Irish heart will be permitted to shew itself in its true light, warm, generous and sincere'.[10]

On 18 May one hundred and seventy 'of the most respectable Protestant Inhabitants' of Belfast 'with a liberality highly creditable to them as Patriots and as Christians' reciprocated Crolly's hospitality by entertaining him to dinner, in what, according to the *Northern Whig*, was a 'genuine tribute of the heart, to a man, whose talents and liberality as a minister, and benevolence as a citizen, had endeared him to his fellow-townsmen'. The *Whig* summed up the pleasant atmosphere of camaraderie and bonhomie of the occasion by declaring that 'there were no features to distinguish the members of one Christian Church from those of another; but Catholic and Protestant all singled like brothers, and vied in promoting the happiness of the evening'.[11]

This goodwill stood Crolly in good stead in the first years of his episcopate. By then the movement for Catholic Emancipation had gained powerful momentum, and in Belfast it found welcome support from Reverend Henry Montgomery, the Presbyterian minister of Derriaghy and a professor in the Belfast Academical Institution. In January 1828 a large meeting in aid of Emancipation was held in St Patrick's Church at which the leading liberals of the town were present. At Crolly's invitation Montgomery spoke. In the evening a dinner of the Friends of Civil and Religious Liberty was held, and Crolly in proposing a toast remarked:

> The liberality of the Presbyterian ministers is interwoven with the records of their religion. I shall select one out of the many excellent ministers belonging to the Synod of Ulster and give you the Reverend H Montgomery and the Synod.[12]

In January 1829 another great meeting was held in St Patrick's Church and Montgomery again addressed it. He referred to the strangeness of the situation: 'a Presbyterian minister standing on a Catholic altar, beside a Catholic prelate, with whom he lived on the most friendly terms, and addressing his Roman Catholic countrymen on the subject of their grievances, was unfortunately, at the present period no ordinary occurrence. How is it', he said, 'that I, who differ so widely from you in my religious sentiments, should be received by you with such testimonies of cordiality and affection, while those who agree most with you in theological opinions are the bitterest enemies of your rights?'[13] He was referring to the theological struggle then taking place in the Presbyterian Church. On the question of submission to creeds and in particular on the issue of the Divinity of Christ Reverend Henry Cooke was the leader of the opposing party which wanted the clergy to subscribe to strict formulas emphasising belief in the Trinity. Cooke won that struggle, and though theologically he was closer to Catholicism, politically he was opposed to it. While prepared to accept Catholic Emancipation he soon came to the conclusion that every Catholic advance meant a Protestant retreat, and he aligned himself with the Church of Ireland and the aristocrats and gentry, the pillars of Toryism in Ireland. Cooke also succeeded in drawing a majority of Presbyterians with him into a political alignment with the Tory forces; Montgomery's wing, which later became known as Non-subscribing Presbyterian, represented a minority in the Presbyterian body, but it was a tough and tenacious one and in general liberally inclined. Montgomery and his like-minded clergy remained friendly with the Catholic community and Montgomery supported plans for reform that would have benefited Catholics, but they parted company on the question of repeal of the union.

Shortly after his appointment to Down and Connor, Crolly obtained permission from Rome to remain in Belfast rather than retain Downpatrick as his mensal parish. He rightly foresaw that Belfast had become the centre of the diocese and, as parish priest, he himself continued to devote as much time as possible to pastoral work there. He also encouraged his clergy throughout the diocese to equip their parishes with churches and Sunday schools, and soon new churches were rising in places where hitherto Catholic communities had been served from a distance. He caused to be printed sufficient copies of Catholic versions of the bible and especially of the New Testament to provide one at a very cheap rate for every Catholic household in the diocese. He supported, and encouraged his clergy to support, the Catholic Book Society which from Dublin undertook to supply parishes with catechisms and books concerned with basic Catholic teaching, and he also fostered the establishment of confraternities of Christian Doctrine to help the clergy instruct the youth of their parishes on Sundays. In 1833 he acquired Vicinage House which was then in the suburbs of Belfast, and therein founded St Malachy's College, as a junior seminary for candidates for the priesthood and a secondary school for boys aspiring to higher education or a career in business or commerce.

II

In 1835 the Archbishop of Armagh died, and the parish priests of the diocese met to select the names of three candidates from whom Rome might choose a successor. During the last vacancy which had occurred in 1817 the clergy of Armagh had striven hard to obtain the primacy for one of their own number. On this occasion forty-six votes were cast: Crolly obtained 29, the Bishop of Kilmore 11 and the parish priest of Dundalk 6.[14] The clergy of Armagh had paid Crolly a fine tribute - not only by choosing him, as a non-Armagh man, but also by giving him such a decided preference. He was duly appointed and when the clergy of Down and Connor heard of this, such was their disappointment that they met and drew up a petition to the Holy See asking that he be allowed to remain with them. But on the advice of the Archbishop of Dublin the petition was not forwarded.[15]

In Armagh Crolly carried on the same busy round of pastoral activity as he had done in Down and Connor. In 1846 he reported to Rome that since his transfer to the archdiocese he had blessed and opened seventeen new churches and that five more would shortly be completed.[16] He took over the parish of Armagh as a mensal parish, and divided his time between it and Drogheda. In 1838 he opened St Patrick's College in Armagh, as a junior seminary for aspirants to the priesthood and for boys who wished to proceed to higher studies or to a career in business. Within a short time he acquired a fine site for a cathedral, and on 17 March 1840 he laid the foundation stone.

III

In 1831 the national system of education was established in Ireland. A board of commissioners was set up in Dublin to disburse the annual grants supplied by parliament. Of its seven members five were Protestants and two Catholic, and among them were both archbishops of Dublin. The central principle of the system was the combining of children of all denominations for moral and literary, and their separation for religious, instruction. Rules were drawn up to ensure that separate religious instruction was given either on one or two days weekly or before or after literary instruction on other days. For the establishment of a new school, a site and one third of the costs had to be found locally, and the board was prepared to look more favourably on applications which came from representatives of both the Protestant and Catholic churches. Provision was also made for the grants of books and school requisites at half price and for the payment of the greater part of teachers' salaries. Soon after its establishment the board started to publish text books for general use and also a series of scripture extracts which were designed for use by children of all denominations.

In general the Catholic reaction to the new system was initially favourable. It promised an acceptable alternative to the schools conducted by the Kildare Place Society which enforced the reading of the scriptures without note or comment. Catholic leaders had long warned their children not to attend the schools run by various proselytising societies. The national system offered a poor and education-hungry people the chance to send their children to schools which were not detrimental to their faith and which were subsidised to a significant extent by the state.

The national system met instant hostility from the established church and from some congregations of the Presbyterian church. The clergy of the established church took the view that they were entitled to control the education of the state, and were also strongly opposed to any limitation on the use of the bible. The Presbyterians likewise objected to limitation on the use of the bible, and to Catholic clergy teaching in schools which they had built, and some of them took strong exception to the Saturdays or popish holidays which were set aside for the teaching of religion. They also repudiated the right of the board to what they claimed was control over books and teachers.

The established church set up its own society and system in 1839 and for about twenty years had sufficient resources to compete against the national system. The Presbyterians opened negotiations with the government and achieved a substantial victory. In non-vested schools, i.e. in those to which the board had not contributed a share of the building costs but had given supplies of books and teachers salaries, permission was granted for religious instruction at any time as long as no child whose parents objected, was obliged to take it.

Catholics, on the other hand, during the first six years of the existence of the system, not only raised no objections to it but connected many of their existing schools with the board and sought its assistance in establishing new schools. The first school in Co Antrim to ask for aid was at Randalstown, and was under the management of Daniel Curoe, the parish priest, and the third school was St Patrick's, Donegall Street, which Crolly had opened in 1829. Crolly himself, thirteen Protestants and twelve Catholics signed this application[17].

Then suddenly and unexpectedly in 1838 Archbishop John MacHale of Tuam launched a campaign against the national system with a public letter to Lord John Russell, the Prime Minister. Crolly promptly called with the Lord Lieutenant to express privately his disapproval of this development.[18] MacHale, however, did not content himself with a display of public hostility to the system; he carried his opposition further afield, in fact, as far as the Pope. Then in a series of letters to the Prefect of Propaganda, the congregation which had charge of Irish ecclesiastical affairs, he referred to the duplicity by which the British government was trying to destroy the faith in Ireland, and pointed out that the government gave money for a mixed system in which all children read scripture extracts that were taken partly from a Catholic version and partly from a Protestant one. Allegedly for reasons of honour and justice but in reality for purposes of deception, a few Catholics were placed on the mainly Protestant commission which selected all books, including religious ones for the schools, and only the bishops chosen by the government for the commission and not those appointed by the Holy See were entrusted with choosing books for use in religious education. Teachers were required to train in a normal school where both Catholic and Protestant came under the influence of a Calvinist rector who, though obliged to keep silent on questions of dogma, had been found to corrupt their minds by interpretations of scripture harmful to faith and morals. The atrocious persecutions of the past, MacHale went on, had ended but by these perfidious means the enemies of the faith were striving to subvert the Catholic Church. If Catholics, he argued, both clerical and lay, were to oppose the corrupting influences of mixed education, the British government would undoubtedly grant money for separate education.[19]

Confronted with such a serious accusation of religious hostility on the part of 'perfidious Albion' the Pope ordered the Congregation of Propaganda to write to MacHale and to Archbishop Murray of Dublin for further information. Murray duly explained the background to the system, pointed out that school patrons were not obliged to use the scripture extracts, quoted a letter he had received from Crolly who had explained that he had found nothing in the system to force him to retract the full and sincere support he had given it.[20] Copies of the scripture lessons were forwarded by MacHale to Rome and in due course a defence and explanation of them by Murray,[21] and they were examined by Roman theologians. In January 1839 the bishops held their annual meeting in Dublin and the controversy over the national schools naturally dominated the discussions. Three resolutions were passed declaring that the system had not damaged the faith or morals of Catholic children, that the board of commissioners merited the confidence of the prelates and that they would watch the system carefully lest any damaging change might be made in it. MacHale was unwilling to accept these terms. He, his suffragans and the bishops of Ardagh, Meath and Ferns wrote to Rome reiterating the objections already made and asking for a verdict from the Pope. Crolly and fifteen other bishops wrote defending the national schools.[22]

Crolly a short time later conveyed his feelings to Paul Cullen, the rector of the Irish College and agent of the Irish bishops in Rome, to be passed on to the appropriate authorities. He wrote:

> With painful feelings, I have to acquaint you, for the information of the Holy See, that an unfortunate misunderstanding among the Prelates of this Kingdom has lately been occasioned by the unwise and obstinate conduct of the Most Reverend Dr MacHale, Archbishop of Tuam, who has determined to use every means in his

power for the purpose of destroying the liberal and impartial system of National Education, which has been prepared by our paternal Government, sanctioned by all the Prelates of the Country including Dr MacHale himself, and the many advantages of which have been enjoyed by the children of Poor Catholics in every part of Ireland during the last seven years.

I need not tell you that, throughout all Ireland, for the last two centuries, the children of the poor of every religious denomination have been educated together in the same Schools, and that owing to the fidelity of the people and the prudent zeal of their pious pastors, this mixed system of education was attended with no injury to Religion; but on the contrary, that the more knowledge the Catholic in general acquired, the more capable they were to assist their pastors in converting those who were separated from the true Church.

The bigoted[23] Protestants plainly perceived that they were constantly losing some members of their communion, and that they could never make proselytes of the poor Catholics, unless they could obtain such a system of education as would enable them to pervert the tender hearts and unsuspecting minds of the poor children. For this impious purpose they obtained from the Tory Government a large grant of money, to enable them to build schools, from which they excluded the Catholic Catechism, and introduced their version of the Bible, which they put into the hands of the pupils, and pointed out many passages of what they called the Word of God, as evidence of the errors of the Catholic Religion. In opposition to this infamous Association of intolerant Protestants, commonly called the Kildare Street Society, the Catholic Prelates, the Clergy and the people made a determined and successful resistance, the children of the faithful were withdrawn from the schools of corruption, and the Kildare Street Society soon sank into a state of insignificance and contempt. This may afford the Holy See a satisfactory proof of our unalterable determination to watch over the faithful flocks entrusted to our care, and to guard them from the insidious attacks of their irreligious inveterate enemies ...

This laudable system of National education has been and still is assailed by all the Bigoted Protestants, whilst it has been received with feelings of inexpressible joy by the Catholic Prelates, who together with their Clergy and their faithful flocks have adopted it in every part of Ireland. By the joint exertions of the Board of Education and the Catholic Clergy, commodious Schoolhouses have been erected in every Province, and almost in every parish throughout Ireland, wherein upwards of two hundred thousand children, who with few exceptions are of the Catholic Communion, are receiving at present such literary knowledge as will make them understand the duties which they should perform as members of Society, and at the same time, they are properly instructed in all the articles of Catholic faith, and all their obligations as members of the Church of Christ ... You will have the goodness to state to His Holiness that the children of the poor in this Country and their indigent parents will be in a miserable and dangerous condition if they be obliged to abandon the national schools, and be once more exposed to the snares of the Kildare Street Society, which would lose no time in renewing their attempts to seduce the Catholic Children from their faith. I fear also that the Catholic Clergy will be deeply mortified and discontented, if they be ordered to abandon the Schools which they have generously and zealously erected at great expense, and under many difficulties. And I cannot conceal from you, that many prudent Prelates are under disagreeable apprehensions, lest this unpleasant business may be attended with a misunderstanding between the Holy See and the British Government which would be injurious to the progress of our holy Religion not only in the British Empire, but also in all the British colonies.[24]

At their meeting in January 1839 both sides decided to appeal to Rome. The cardinals of Propaganda considered the material submitted to them and in July 1839 decided formally on a condemnation.[25] This decision did not, of course, take effect until confirmed by the Pope, but because of a passionate appeal from the Archbishop of Dublin which reached him at that time the Pope decided to postpone ratification until the issue was studied at greater length.

Rome then wrote to both groups within the hierarchy asking them to send out a priest to Rome to explain their cases.[26] Crolly duly agreed with the Archbishop of Dublin that their side should be represented by two Dublin priests. He also submitted to Rome statements from his parish priests in praise of their system, in which they recalled the pressure applied to their children to go to Protestant schools before the national system was instituted.[27] When the bishops met again in 1840 further attempts were made to reach a compromise and terms were presented to the Viceroy on which all the prelates could agree, but he refused to alter the basic rules of the system.

The agent of the majority in Rome asked that the bishops be allowed to accept or reject the system according to the dictates of their own consciences, and this was what cardinals agreed to do when they considered the issue on 22 December 1840. They demanded some safeguards: all books which contained any material of a dangerous nature from a religious point of view were to be removed from the schools; bishops and parish priests were exhorted to be vigilant to prevent the system from causing any harm to Catholic students, and were encouraged to obtain legal ownership of the schools.[28] The majority had won. The national system survived and was allowed to expand even in the dioceses of bishops who had opposed it, apart from Tuam.

Though Crolly and Murray led the winning side in the dispute over the national schools, they were less successful in the other struggles which engaged episcopal energies during the 1840s. Neither of them supported the Repeal Movement which Daniel O'Connell organised with enormous skill and which by 1843 enjoyed the enthusiastic support of the majority of the bishops. Crolly probably believed that Repeal was unattainable and divisive; even his friend, the liberal-minded Presbyterian, Henry Montgomery, strongly objected to it, and the majority of Presbyterians for whom Henry Cooke spoke, together with their allies in the established church, were inexorably opposed to any constitutional change in the relationship of Ireland to Britain. The primate's aloofness from the campaign was anything but popular, and helps to explain some of the animus to which he was subjected in the dispute over other issues.

The first of these disputes concerned charitable bequests. To update and regularise arrangements about wills for charitable purposes an act was passed in 1844 which, among other things, established a new body of commissioners to oversee all matters connected with legacies left to charities. The act was passed by the Tory government at a time of great political tension. O'Connell's campaign for repeal had been going very successfully, attracting increasing support and promising to be as successful as the campaign for Catholic Emancipation until the government banned the monster-meeting that was due to be held at Clontarf in October 1843. O'Connell accepted the ban, and to make matters worse, he and a group of close supporters were shortly afterwards imprisoned and tried for treason. Catholic Ireland in 1844 was not in a receptive mood and the charitable bequests act contained two clauses which were to produce much dissension: bequests made within three months of the testator's death were not valid, and religious orders, which had been penalised by the Catholic Emancipation Act, were not recognised as recipients of bequests.

The act provoked a tremendous uproar among both Catholic

clergy and laity. It was depicted as a revival of the penal code and public meetings were called throughout the country to denounce it. The government invited Crolly, Murray and Bishop Denvir of Down and Connor to join the board which was to administer the act. They did so, chiefly on the grounds that whatever flaws the new legislation contained, it was a big improvement on the previous system. They were, however, roundly denounced for their pains, and MacHale and some of his allies charged that as commissioners the three bishops had no right to concern themselves with any ecclesiastical matters that were connected with other dioceses.

Sharp as were the divisions caused by this piece of legislation, they were not nearly as serious as those caused by the Academical Colleges Act. In May 1845 the government introduced a bill to establish colleges for third-level education, especially in arts, law and medicine, to cater for Catholics and Presbyterians who were not served by Trinity College, Dublin, which was closely linked with the established church. A sum of £100,000 was set aside for capital costs with a pledge of £6,000 to each college annually to cover current expenditure. The bill proposed to vest all professorial appointments in the crown and, to ensure religious neutrality in the colleges, chairs of theology were excluded though provision was made for the private endowment of divinity. The colleges were quickly denounced as 'Godless' on all sides, and Crolly called a meeting of bishops to discuss the new arrangements, which, he told them, were pregnant with danger to the faith and morals of their youth. The bishops at their meeting on 21 May drew up a memorial asking that a fair proportion of the staff should be Catholic, that a board of trustees, of which the bishops of the provinces where the colleges were situated would be members, would appoint and dismiss, would be salaried by the colleges and that a Catholic professor would be appointed to the chairs of logic, metaphysics, moral philosophy, history, geology and anatomy.[29] The Lord Lieutenant told the deputation of four bishops, including Crolly, who presented this memorial to him, that the government would stand firm on principle but that changes could be introduced when the charters and laws of the colleges were being drawn up. The government went ahead and passed the bill within three months of its introduction.

Definite locations had not been chosen for the colleges when the royal assent was given, and so some of the leading citizens of Armagh resolved to stake their claim to the northern college. A meeting was arranged in the city on 7 August 1845. Reference was made to the ancient ecclesiastical schools of Armagh and to the valuable public library and the Royal Observatory, which would be of great help to future students. Crolly, who was present, explained that the amendments that had been made to the bill ensured that no student would be received into any of the colleges unless he would lodge with his parent, a relative, a guardian or in a house duly licensed by the president of the college. And the provision that had been made for chaplains to superintend the moral conduct of their students had also reassured him. Consequently, he thought their provincial college should be given a fair trial, and this could best be done by having it in Armagh in the centre of the province. He moved that a committee should be appointed to draw up a memorial to the Viceroy in favour of Armagh. He himself was duly chosen as one of the seven-member committee[30].

What seems to have changed his views on the colleges was an assurance from government sources that halls of residence for students forced to live away from home could be licensed and supervised by a chaplain or dean. Probably he foresaw a small number of Catholic students, maybe 25 or 35, attending the college in Armagh and planned 'o extend St Patrick's College or acquire adjacent property to house them. However, to MacHale and his party, Crolly's behaviour was quite incomprehensible; they saw in it the unilateral betrayal of their body by its head. The *Pilot*, O'Connell's Repeal paper, which was not well disposed to the Archbishop of Armagh took advantage of this seeming volte-face on the colleges to subject him to a base personal insult. Shortly after the Armagh meeting when the Archbishop was forced for personal reasons to miss a meeting at Maynooth, the *Pilot* suggested that the balance of his mind was disturbed. The clergy of Armagh reacted vigorously to this foul accusation and published statements in the papers denouncing what they called 'a slanderous and unprincipled article, which was also a cowardly and sacrilegious libel on the character of the pious and faithful head of the Catholic Church in Ireland'.[31]

The issue of the colleges dominated the annual meeting of the bishops, which took place in November. By then protest meetings had been held in many dioceses and Catholic public opinion was swinging strongly against them. At the end of two days of debate a motion was proposed by MacHale charging that the government had not granted the securities that the bishops had required and therefore demanding that the bishops' original resolution (of May) and the grounds on which they were based should be submitted to the judgement of the Pope. Crolly and Murray wanted further evidence to be submitted. Of the eighteen bishops present a large majority supported the Archbishop of Tuam's plan.

A week later MacHale, Archbishop Slattery of Cashel and fifteen other bishops set out their objections at length in a letter to Rome and begged the Holy See to give judgement on the issue; if the proposed system ever became a reality, they claimed, the gravest of evils that would be beyond subsequent remedy would arise. They maintained that a Protestant Queen and her successors had exclusive control of the appointments of staff, they objected to the authorities of the colleges having any connection with the appointment of chaplains and they distrusted the arrangements made for the accommodation of students. The whole system, deriving from a tainted source, endangered the faith and morals of Catholic students.

On the same day Crolly, Murray and four other bishops also wrote to Rome. They pointed out that two of the presidents of the three colleges had already been appointed; one was a distinguished Catholic doctor and the other a parish priest, who held a doctorate in theology. Recalling the munificence of the government to Maynooth and the attempts to proselytise Catholic youth at Trinity College, Dublin, they argued that suitable and safe accommodation would be provided for the students and that the bishops could appoint chaplains to look after their spiritual welfare.[32]

Consultors were requested by the Roman authorities to examine all the documentation submitted. On 13 July 1846 the cardinals decided that a letter should be sent to the bishops of Ireland which, while acknowledging that those who favoured the colleges were motivated only by a desire to further the interests of religion, would nonetheless declare that the colleges were dangerous, and that the bishops should have nothing to do with them. The hierarchy of Ireland was encouraged to increase the number of Catholic Colleges.[33]

The new pope, Pius IX, who had been elected less than a month before this decision was taken, was in no hurry to promulgate it, and in fact it was not promulgated until a year later. The rescript condemning the colleges and urging the bishops to set up their own university on the model of Louvain was dated 9 October 1847.[34] This verdict must have come as a body blow to Crolly. He had gone further than other members of the minority party, for he had supported the establishment of a college in Armagh. Now he stood implicitly rebuked in the eyes of the whole Catholic community. Three weeks later Crolly replied to the Roman letter. While promising obedience, he indicated that he did not regard the rescript as a final and irrevocable judgement. He then took issue with two of the recommendations made in the rescript - the enlargement of the diocesan colleges and the establishment of a Catholic university - by pointing out that the Catholic colleges or seminaries were geared to students preparing for the priesthood and by insisting that the church in Ireland had neither the resources to enlarge and endow them or to fund a university on the model of Louvain. She was completely incapable of providing the sums of money required - either in capital or running costs.[35] In this letter Crolly put his finger unerringly on the basic weakness of the Roman recommendations: the confusion about the nature of the colleges and the virtual impossibility of finding the resources among the Catholics of Ireland to build, sustain and staff a Catholic university. There could not have been a more unpropitious time to make recommendations about spending money on a Catholic university than in the autumn of 1847; the struggle to survive amidst famine and disease engaged the energies of most Irish people at that time.

The new Lord Lieutenant, Lord Clarendon, who arrived in Ireland in May 1847, was anxious to make the colleges work and, without altering the act of parliament, hoped to draw up the statutes in such a way as to win the backing of Crolly, Murray and ultimately Rome. This he did by making regulations whereby students would reside either in a hostel under the control of their chaplain or in a house approved by him, by laying down that the archbishop and bishop of the province where the colleges were situated would be visitors empowered to investigate the discipline and possible breaches of rules in the colleges and by imposing obligations on the staff not to teach anything contrary to the religious beliefs of any of their students. These statutes were forwarded to Rome and a couple of agents - Francis Joseph Nicholson, the Coadjutor Archbishop of Corfu, and John Ennis, a priest of the diocese of Dublin - went to Rome as advocates for the colleges. However, not to be outdone Archbishop MacHale and one of his closest allies, the Bishop of Ardagh, also went to Rome to put their case. A good deal more documentation landed on the desks of the Roman officials. However, when the cardinals met again to discuss the issue in September 1848 they saw no reason to change their minds. The second rescript reaffirmed the first. Stating that the revised statutes and opinions of the bishops on them had been considered, it pointed out that the Holy See was unable to change its previous decision 'on account of the grievous and intrinsic dangers of the same Colleges'. The bishops were again exhorted to found a Catholic university and were encouraged to work together in harmony.[36]

This strife about the Queen's Colleges took place against one of the saddest backgrounds in the history of Ireland. From 1845 to 1849 the country was ravaged by famine, and hunger and its accompanying fevers carried off perhaps a million people. The bishops, priests and indeed many clergy of all denominations strove to succour their people by organising relief at every level. The worst hit areas were along the western and southern seaboards but poorer parts of the Archdiocese of Armagh experienced serious suffering and loss. Crolly did his best to organise and channel relief funds. In what was to be the last year of the famine the country was also struck by cholera and the general weakness of many people after enduring such great hardships meant that their resistance was low and made them easy victims. Among these victims was the Archbishop of Armagh. Struck down on Holy Thursday, he died the following day, Good Friday, 6 April 1849.

There was a striking and strangely fitting poignancy both in the manner and timing of his death: the primate, like so many of his co-religionists, suddenly carried off by fever and that on the same day as the death of the Lord whom he had so faithfully and wholeheartedly tried to serve.

ABBREVIATIONS

AICR   Archives of the Irish College, Rome

APF   Archives of the Congregation of Propaganda Fide, Rome

PRO   Public Record Office, London

PRONI   Public Record Office of Northern Ireland, Belfast

BNL   *Belfast News Letter*

Ir   *Irishman*

NW   *Northern Whig*

NOTES

1. This is a slightly altered version of the Canon Rogers Memorial lecture which was given in St Mary's College, Belfast on 5 February 1990.
2. BNL 7 Mar 1815
3. Ibid 10 Mar 1815
4. Minutes of the General and Committee Meetings of the Belfast Society for Promoting Knowledge, pp 6-9, 54-55 (Linen Hall Library, Belfast)
5. Fourth Report of the Commissioners of Irish Education Inquiry HC 1826-27, (89), xiii, 180-3
6. BNL 11 July 1815
7. NW 22 July 1824
8. Ir 30 July, 6 Aug 1824, BNL 30 July, 3 Aug, 13 Aug 1824
9. Ir 6 Aug 1824
10. NW 5 May 1825
11. Ibid 19 May 1825
12. Ibid 17 Jan 1828
13. J A Crozier, *The Life of the Rev Henry Montgomery* (London 1875) pp246-7
14. APF *Acta* 198, ff 11r-112v
15. Denvir to Cullen 28 June 1836 AICR
16. Crolly to Cullen 26 June 1846 Ibid
17. PRONI ED1/1/3
18. Lord Mulgrave to Lord John Russell, 18 Feb 1838 PRO 30/22/3A ff 130-1. According to Mulgrave Crolly 'volunteered to express his entire disapprobation' of MacHale's first letter and went on to describe MacHale as '*our* Bishop of Exeter'. The Anglican Bishop

of Exeter was a well-known evangelical extremist.
19. APF *Acta* 202 ff 209r-212v
    The letters are dated 1 July, 3 Nov and 7 Dec 1838
20. Murray to Propaganda 11 June 1838 Ibid ff 214v-216v
21. Ibid 25 Feb and 12 Mar 1839 ff 219v-228v
22. Ibid ff 213r-214v and 230v-231r. The letters were dated 29 Jan and 30 Jan 1839
23. This refers to those extreme Protestants who sought to use education as a means of proselytism, not to Protestants in general.
24. Crolly to Cullen 4 Feb 1839 AICR
25. APF *Acta* 202 f 208rv
26. Propaganda to Murray and MacHale 7 Sept 1838, Ibid ff 415r-416r
27. APF SOCG 958 ff 100r-103r. These statements were compiled and signed by the clergy who attended the conferences which were held at Armagh, Dunleer, Dungannon and Dundalk in October 1839
28. APF *Acta* 203 ff 412r-413r
29. F McGrath *Newman's University, Idea and Reality* (Dublin 1951) pp 45-6. There is a full discussion of the 'Godless Colleges' for the period 1845-6 in A Kerr *Peel, Priests and Politics* (Oxford 1982) pp 290-351
30. NW 14 Aug 1845
31. Ibid 11 Oct 1845
32. APF *Acta* 209 ff 289r-293r and 198r-299r. The letters were dated 24 and 25 Nov 1845
33. Ibid ff 355rv
34. Ibid *Acta* 211 ff 359r-360r and McGrath Op Cit pp 63-4
35. Crolly to Propaganda 5 Nov 1847, APF *Acta* 211 ff 360v-361v
36. The rescript was published in the *Freeman's Journal* of 26 Oct 1848, where it was described as 'a charter of religion, of liberty and of independence'.

ENTERPRISE, INDUSTRIAL DEVELOPMENT AND SOCIAL PLANNING: QUAKERS AND THE EMERGENCE OF THE TEXTILE INDUSTRY IN IRELAND

by Arthur P. Williamson

This article examines two Quaker industrial settlements in Ireland which were developed in the early and mid-nineteenth century. It throws new light on the origins of the model housing movement and on Quaker preoccupation with the concept of the ideal industrial community in the context of the beginnings of industrialization in Ireland. The second part of the article considers the founders of Portlaw and Bessbrook in the light of what may be learned of their motivation and of the social philosophies which would have shaped their approach to enterprise, industrial development and social planning. Linkages with New Lanark and other influences on the Irish developments are explored and suggested influences on Cadbury's celebrated experiment at Bournville are discussed.

Introduction

The Industrial Revolution in Ireland had its earliest concentration in two valleys on the east coast: the Lagan in Ulster and the Lower Suir near Waterford in the south. Power-driven technology, first using water and then steam, affected the milling of flour and later the production of textiles. Both valleys were the location of major industrial enterprises and social experiments. In each case Quaker acumen, enterprise and social philosophy were major factors.

The first settlement, begun in 1818 by David Malcolmson (1765-1844), was situated at Portlaw in Co. Waterford; the second was established in 1845 at Bessbrook in Co. Armagh by John G. Richardson (JGR), a close relative of the Malcolmsons. Although it was well known in the nineteenth century, the Portlaw development has now been largely forgotten. The Richardson's social experiment at Bessbrook is today much better remembered. It was also widely known by contemporaries and may have influence, George Cadbury when, a generation later, he planned Bournville. Writing of Bessbrook, J.S. Curl has said that the work of the Richardsons was of 'great importance in the nineteenth century reform movement'. Curl considered that Richardson's work was 'an example to Cadbury and pre-dates Saltaire, Victoria and all the famous mid-Victorian model villages and towns'[1].

By contrast with England where widespread industralization was taking place by the end of the eighteenth century, in Ireland it was not until the second part of the nineteenth century that industries began to take some of the surplus population off the land. Portlaw and Bessbrook are therefore of additional interest as they were some of the earliest settlements of the industrial revolution in Ireland. Each was located in a rural area and became a sort of social experiment involving industrial development in undeveloped countryside. At Portlaw many of those employed and housed were evicted cottiers cleared from their small holdings by absentee English landlords.

It is important to place Portlaw and Bessbrook in context for, although they were the largest and the most successful, they were not the only new communities being developed in Ireland in this period. In Ulster in the late eighteenth century at Lisburn several Quaker mill owners carried out experiments with model housing. At Ballitore in Co. Kildare, where, according to the school roll held in the records of the Dublin Friends' Yearly Meeting, J.G. Richardson and the younger David Malcolmson were attending the Quaker school in 1824, there was an experimental housing development.

The Quakers were distinguished for their relief efforts during the catastrophic famine, the 'great hunger' of the later 1840s. Their relief committee distributed money and goods to the value of some £200,000, including 10,000 tons of food and clothing sent by American Friends. But their efforts were not confined to relief. A further Irish Quaker initiative in social planning took place during the famine when a model farm was established in a deprived rural area at Colmanstown, Co. Galway. A large amount of land was reclaimed and improved agricultural methods were introduced. This experiment lasted for nearly 20 years before coming to an end in 1863[2].

Portlaw was established while Robert Owen's New Lanark was being developed. Bessbrook existed before Saltaire (begun in 1851), Bromborough (begun in 1853) or Akroyd's Copeley and Akroydon (begun in 1849 and 1859 respectively). In Ireland Richardson was experimenting with model houses when, in 1850, Lord Shaftesbury's Society was building the model houses in London's Streatham Street which were exhibited at the Great Exhibition the following year. The experiments in employer housing conducted by Malcolmson and Richardson long antedated those of Lever at Port Sunlight, Cadbury at Bournville and Rowntree at New Earswick at the turn of the century.

Over nearly half a century, and spanning several generations, the

Malcolmsons of Portlaw and the Richardsons had family ties through marriage. David Malcolmson had 11 children including seven sons. In August 1839, David, his ninth son, came to Lisburn in Co. Antrim and married Sarah Richardson, daughter of James M. Richardson (1782-1847), a Quaker from Ulster and father of John Grubb Richardson, founder, in 1845, of the Bessbrook mills and village. David died in November of the following year; two months later, Sarah gave birth to a daughter, Anna. She was to marry Henry Barcroft, a director of the Bessbrook mills and inventor of the 'Bessbrook', a machine for weaving damask which marked a significant breakthrough in damask manufacture. A further link between the families was the marriage between JGR's son, James N. Richardson and Sophia Malcolmson, a daughter of William Malcolmson. They settled in Mountcaulfield in 1867[3]. Through educatiion and marriage John Grubb Richardson (1815-90) continued and developed the family's close and long-standing links with the south of Ireland.

John Bellers, William Penn and the antecedents of Quaker planning philosophies

The experience and contribution to planning knowledge of the Irish Quakers is important. The 'dynamic' communities of the great Quaker ironmasters elsewhere in Britain, at Swalewell, Ebbw Vale and Coalbrookdale would have been well known by Malcolmson and Richardson. Less known today, but also certain to have been highly influential, was John Bellers (b.1654), author of *Proposals for raising a College of Industry of all useful trades and husbandry*, in whom Karl Marx and the German social student, Eduard Bernstein, were keenly interested. Bellers, considered to be the earliest Quaker social thinker and philanthropist, was described by Marx as a 'veritable phenomenon in the history · of political economy'[4]. Arguing that 'industry brings plenty' Bellers proposed an elaborate plan for establishing a regulated community work colony of three hundred persons which would contain a balance of industries and agriculture. The community would provide education and social facilities including a library, 'a physic garden for the understanding of herbs and a laboratory for the preparing of medicines'.

Bellers was writing at about the same time as the Quaker theologian from Scotland, Robert Barclay who, together with William Penn and a number of Scotsmen in 1682, was a proprietor of a Quaker settlement in America at East Jersey. The son of a Cromwellian colonel, Barclay broke with Presbyterianism and became a Quaker in Aberdeen in 1666. Though remaining at home and acting in America through a deputy, he was governor of the colony. At the age of 28 Barclay wrote his *Apology for True Christian Divinity* which has been compared with Calvin's *Institutes*. More than any other Quaker writer, he laid the foundations of Quaker theology. His career epitomized the blend of theology and social concern which has ever since characterized the Quakers.

Penn and other leading Quakers were interested in Bellers' plan which he developed over many years. In 1723 he addressed Parliament on it. During his life his plan inspired a number of social and industrial experiments including one at Bristol and another at Clerkenwell, London. His ideas were later taken up by the radical reformer, Francis Place, who discovered Bellers' *Proposals* (1695, 1696), while rearranging his library and brought them to Robert Owen. Owen had them reprinted in 1818 and circulated 1000 copies, one of which he presented to the British Museum. The interest of Marx and Eduard Bernstein has ensured that Bellers' proposals have not been forgotten; indeed they were subsequently reprinted in 1916[5].

When Malcolmson and Richardson were receiving their education the colonizing work of William Penn in America would have been well known to their teachers. As a young man Penn had lived in Ireland where his father had been granted estates by Cromwell. He had become a Quaker there, probably at the time of George Fox's visit in 1658[6]. Malcolmson and Richardson would also have known about his work in planning and designing the city of Philadelphia. There were close links between Pennsylvania and the Irish Quakers and it was a Waterford Quaker, Thomas Holme, like Penn's father a settler in Ireland under Cromwell, whom Penn chose as his surveyor-general to design and execute the building of Philadelphia. Penn and Holme drew on Irish colonizing experience in the design of Pennsylvania and adapted the fortified model of town development used by the English in Ireland as part of their plan of conquest. Garvan suggests that Holme may have known of Raven's plan for the fortified city of Londonderry[7]. It is likely that this in turn had been influenced by earlier English experience in south-west France where the bastide towns were an essential part of the English military stategy in the thirteenth century.

Around 1750 there were some 100 Quaker meeting houses in Ireland. By the end of the century Quakers had become an influential group in the milling industry in the lower Suir Valley in the south-east. Clonmel was at that time a centre of the textile trade, including wool and worsted cloth, and had also emerged as the largest flour milling centre in Ireland. Some of the Clonmel Quakers were interested in social experiments and one of their number, Robert Grubb, possibly inspired by Bellers, was involved in planning a work colony in the Loire Valley in France. Together with Jean Marsillac of Congenies, and with the support of English friends, Grubb applied to the council of the French departement of Loire et Cher for permission to establish an industrial, commercial and artistic community, together with a school in the castle of Chambord. This community, to house 80 or 100 workshops, would have as its aim to introduce new trades and 'particular cultures possessed until now by England'. Despite the welcome of the minister of the interior the scheme had to be abandoned due to the outbreak of war[8].

The Malcolmson family and the development of Portlaw, Co. Waterford

In 1785 Sarah Grubb of Clonmel, Co. Tipperary, advertised through the Quaker meetings in Ireland for 'competent clerks to aid in the administration of her late husband's estates'[9]. She employed David Malcolmson (1765-1844) who came south from the Lagan valley near Belfast in Ulster at the age of 20 to manage her flour mills. Malcolmson was the grandson of a Scottish emigrant, Andrew, who became a leading Presbyterian layman in the small congregation at Lurgan in Co. Armagh. Quaker influence came into the Malcolmson family through marriage with the family of Thomas Greer of Dungannon, a leading Quaker linen merchant. This influence was consolidated in 1795 when David Malcolmson married Mary Ffennell of Cahir, Co. Tipperary, daughter of a leading Quaker family.

Working for Sarah Grubb, Malcolmson was a benevolent employer. When his parents died he received a legacy of £300 which he invested in business interests of his own in the Waterford area. These came eventually to include corn mills at Clonmel, Carrick-on-Suir and Waterford, and a calico factory at Clonmel. Milling of cereals was his major interest, however, and Malcolmson feared changes in the English corn laws which would ruin his corn trade; consequently he decided, on the basis of advice from James Capper, a Quaker preacher, to diversify into cotton.

He bought Mayfield House at Portlaw including about 16 acres of

land, the site of a burnt-out mill and rights to the Coldagh river. It has
been thought that the corn mill was on the site of an iron mill furnace
founded by Robert Boyle, Great Earl of Cork in the seventeenth
century. In a letter to Richard Usher of Dungarvan in April 1825,
Malcolmson explained that he expected to 'make out a fall of about
fourteen feet on which we are prepared to erect a cotton spinning mill.
We have got a most eligible situation'. He had no illusions about the
extent of the commitment which would be required, confessing that:

> We are all about us strangers to the business and if we succeed we
> expect to lay the foundations for employing many thousands of
> people of the country (who now much want it) and if we fail we
> must submit to a serious loss but which we expect to be able to bear
> up against.

Prior to 1818 Portlaw was an inconsequential village on the banks
of the River Clodagh near a large estate owned by the Marquis of
Waterford. Building commenced in 1825 with the south end of the
factory. When the complex was completed it was bigger than the two
biggest mills in Belfast. Eventually the spinning division was 268 feet
long, 47 feet wide and 72 feet high, comprising six storeys. There was
also a one-storey weaving house covering one acre on the west side of
the site. Half of the roof of this building was of glass to give light for
the weavers. Building work continued at a rapid pace and the *Clonmel
Advertiser* reported on 30 July 1825 that the cotton factory 'is at a
very advanced state and when finished at least £15,000 will have been
expended'.

Within ten years Malcolmson had spent £60,000 developing his
Portlaw factory; it was employing some 1000 workers and exporting
32,000 pieces of finished cotton each week. Malcolmson's first
employees had been 'imported Englishmen' but he found that
'Irishmen, being properly instructed, were just as expert'. By the
mid-1830s it was the site of the largest cotton mill in Ireland and in
1847 Portlaw possessed 29% of the cotton spinning jennies in Ireland.
Raw cotton was mainly imported via Liverpool and, when manufactured, it was bleached on the premises. Most of the output was sold on
the home market, although from time to time large quantities were
exported to America. By 1852 weekly output had increased to 120,000
yards of calico representing 42,000 pounds of cotton.

From the start Malcolmson combined water and steam power. By
1838 his steam engines were generating 120 h.p. and the watermills
were producing 200 h.p. This was increased after Malcolmson's

retirement in 1837. In 1838 Lewis reported that the factory's powerful modern machinery was propelled by three large water wheels and three steam engines. By 1850 power production had increased to 500 h.p. It had been necessary to build a canal of about half a mile in length to link the factory with the River Suir. This ran under the receiving house for the factory bringing coal, raw cotton and machinery.

The workers' village established by Malcolmson at Portlaw consisted of broad streets of long rows of cottages. The houses were roofed with Malcolmson's tarred felt roofing and radiated from a large square containing a post office, a playing field and a men's recreation room. It is possible that the design of the square may have been influenced by Jeremy Bentham's *Panopticon* of which there was a Dublin edition in 1791. Bentham had been involved with William Allen and Robert Owen at New Lanark. Shortly before Malcolmson expanded by building a new and larger factory in 1825, an observer of the Irish scene, S.C. Hall, writing about his tour of Ireland, reported that 'the experiment [at Portlaw] has been eminently successful'. In 1830 Henry Inglis wrote that the factories had given useful employment to evicted smallholders 'whose conditions have been rendered superior to what it had ever been'. In 1837 Lewis reported in his *Topographical Dictionary* that a Doctor Martin had been appointed at Portlaw at £100 per annum with apartments and that a school for eighty to one hundred boys and girls employing five to seven teachers had been established inside the factory gates in a hall with dimensions of 60 feet by 30 feet which was available in the evenings for discussions and lectures. The report of the factory inspectors for 1849 recognizes and commends the quality and extent of social provision which had been made for the workers[10.] The provision of a factory doctor must be seen against the background of the fact that Ireland already had a national system of dispensary doctors providing residual medical care to the poor without cost.

By 1837 465 houses had been built, many of which were 'handsome and well built and the remainder small cottages roofed with slates'[11]. Some of these houses are still occupied today and their high standard of design is evident. Each room had a fireplace; all the rooms in the single storey houses had ceilings of twelve feet in height. In 1842 the Inspector of Factories, James Stewart, reported after visiting Portlaw, that the proprietors have spared no pains to provide for the health and comfort of the workpeople by having the apartments of the factory large and well ventilated and ... by the erection of excellent dwelling houses let at moderate rents to the persons they employ but subject regularly to inspections in point of cleanliness and sanitary surveillance as to their habits.[12]

During the decade 1831-41, the population of Portlaw more than doubled, the 1841 census indicating a population of 3647. By mid-century Portlaw employed 1800 workers rising to some 2500 during the American Civil War. Four categories of houses were built by the firm to accommodate the influx:

1. Two bedroom houses with sitting room, parlour and kitchen: rent per annum £5.8.0. (£5.40).

2. Slated two or three bedroom houses with kitchen: rent per annum £3.12.0. (£3.60).

3. Thatched houses with kitchen and two bedrooms: rent per annum £3.0.0. (£3.00).

4. Slated houses with one bedroom and a kitchen: rent per annum £2.8.0. (£2.40).

The company kept the houses in repair and in the 1830s the rents were some 30% lower than those paid to other owners for similar houses. In 1841 virtually all the rented houses in Portlaw were valued in the Poor Law valuation at a figure below what was being charged for their rent.

With regard to other features of the village, in 1839 when the temperance movement was still in its infancy, Portlaw inhabitants formed a Tontine Club which had the joint purpose of promoting temperance and saving. Membership was confined to the employees of the company. Together with the Mayfield Provident Society, the Tontine Club was well supported by the workers. The Society is an early example of an industrial self-help movement providing cash support in cases of death or disability. Weekly contributions entitled the employee to benefits ranging from two to 16 shillings (10-80p) for the first four months with a reduction of 50% thereafter, the amount being determined by the level of contribution and paid on condition that the illness or accident was not caused by 'drunkenness, debauchery, rioting, quarrelling etc.' The rules of the Mayfield Provident Society were reprinted by J. F. Maguire in 1853[13].

By 1865 the Malcolmson company owned some 322 houses of the 600 in the village. In that year Dr. E. D. Mapother, Medical Officer of Health for Dublin, gave a paper to the Social and Statistical Society of Ireland concerning the need for improved public health legislation and housing bye laws in Ireland. He attributed the cause to the foresightedness of the Malcolmson family and drew attention to the superior state of health of the residents of Portlaw, in spite of the fact that Portlaw had not adopted a towns act, and although it had a population of 3892 persons. Mapother found that the houses provided by the Malcolmsons at Portlaw were of a better standard of construction and with superior sanitary facilities compared with other houses in Portlaw. The Malcolmson houses were:

> clean and comfortable ... [with] preventable diseases [being] one
> fourth less frequent in them than in the remaining 278 squalid houses
> of the town[14].

On his retirement in 1837 David Malcolmson was succeeded as senior partner by his eldest son, Joseph, marking the end of the firm of David Malcolmson and Sons and inaugurating the era of Malcolmson Brothers. It is difficult to determine the influences which may have guided David Malcolmson in connection with the development of the community at Portlaw. Less is known about him than about his relative, J. G. Richardson. His ideas of community were in all probability much less developed. The passage cited above shows that he had a concern to provide employment for displaced cottiers; the reports of visitors to Portlaw show that it possessed workers' housing of remarkably high quality. It is likely that the development of the Tontine Club and of the Portlaw Provident Society were encouraged by the company.

As suggested earlier it is likely that Malcolmson would have known of Penn's experiments in planning in America. He would also have known Robert Grubb of Clonmel. It is not inconceivable that he might have participated in discussions about the plans for Grubb's industrial, commercial and artistic community in the Loire valley in France. And he would certainly have known of the experiments with improved housing for workers which had been carried out at Lisburn and at Ballitore. As host to William Allen on his visits to Ireland, he would certainly have been acquainted with Allen's magazine, *The Philanthropist or repository of hints and suggestions calculated to promote the comfort and happiness of man* which had begun publication in 1811.

The Nicholson and Richardson families and the development of Bessbrook

Bessbrook is situated 40 miles from Belfast and some three miles north-west of Newry in a valley in which flax growing was one of the staple activities and which had been long established as a centre of linen bleaching. The origins of Bessbrook and of its linen trade are obscure. It is, however, known that linen was being manufactured there as early as 1761 by the Pollock family who sold their interests to the Nicholson family in 1802. From that date until 1845, using the rapid flow of the Camlough river as a source of power, Bessbrook became a centre for the wet spinning method developed by James Kay of Preston in 1825, and in 1827 the Irish Linen Board granted the Nicholsons £600 for spinning by Kay's process. Wet spinning led to the expansion of the mechanized factory system; manufacturers no longer had to locate near water power and increasingly used steam power produced from coal[15]. In its heyday the Bessbrook mills consumed 10,000 tons of coal each year, brought from the port of Newry by the firm's hydro-electric powered tramway.

The Richardson family came to Ireland in the reign of James I, and is thought to be one of the oldest of the linen trade pioneers. In 1660, through the preaching of William Edmundson, Jonathan Richardson became a member of the Society of Friends in company with the Nicholsons of Co. Armagh and a number of other families including the Greers of Dungannon and the Grubbs of Co. Tipperary. Jonathan Richardson's three grandchildren all married into the Nicholson family who were in the linen trade and who had, by 1805, built the first power (dry spinning) mill in Ireland.

A later Jonathan (born 1756) purchased two bleach greens at Lisburn in Co. Antrim known as Glenmore bleach greens, where he originated winter bleaching in 1800. His son, James Nicholson Richardson, (1782-1847), developed his father's business, increasing his wealth through marriage to Anna Grubb of Clonmel, Co. Tipperary in 1810. They had seven sons including John Grubb and Jonathan. J. N. Richardson was joined in his business in 1825 by John Owden, a young Englishman of French Huguenot descent, and the firm traded as J. N. Richardson, Sons and Owden.

In the late 1830s JGR emerged as the senior partner in the firm. In 1838 he and two of his brothers founded the firm of Richardson

Brothers and Co. of Belfast; they opened an office in Liverpool and, in 1841, a branch in New York which was supervised by JGR's younger brother, Thomas.

In 1837 the Nicholson mill at Bessbrook employed 180 persons in spinning linen and yarn[16]. The mill burned down in 1839 and was offered for sale in the *Northern Whig* newspaper in August 1844 as a valuable site, 'with water power ... 50 acres of land with residence, buildings and workmen's houses for an extensive factory'. The brothers, Jonathan and JGR, together with their ailing father and John Owden, wanting to develop their business by becoming spinners and finishers, purchased the site for a mill. Until that time, they had principally bleached brown cloth bought in the market, but changing trends in the industry obliged the firm to keep pace with the times and become flax spinners and manufacturers.

In 1846 JGR began to build his factory and undertake the social experiment which incorported his ideas of community. At that time Bessbrook was virtually a green field site. During the first 20 years expansion was steady. The site was partly on the side of a hill and the village was laid out 'so that all the advantages of high elevation might be secured without any of the troublesome drawbacks created from steep descents'[17]. Central to the village were two squares with open greens lined with solid granite facades of houses for which stone was obtained from a quarry nearby.

The first building at Bessbrook was 'Just a small mill with a flat roof in the middle of a green'. Spinning probably began in the last few months of 1846 and from that time development was rapid and continuous. In 1849 work began on the Time House and it appears that the principal buildings of the main hall, which were five storeys high, were begun about the same time. Of dressed granite, they were eventually extended to a frontage of 660 feet.

The Quaker diarist, Caroline Fox, visited Bessbrook in 1852 in connection with her attendance at the British Association meeting in Belfast. She wrote of a 'flourishing village ... with its immense linen factory, beautiful schools and model houses for workmen'[18]. Fountain Street, running in front of the flax spinning and weaving mills was the first development of workers' houses, one up, one down stone buildings of 12 foot frontage with open hearths and dry closets known as 'salt box' houses on account of their single pitch slate roof. Fountain Street was followed by Charlemont Square East, built in 1855. Whereas the earlier houses closely resembled existing rural labourers' housing, the Charlemont Square houses were built to much higher specifications. They represented the beginnings of an attempt by JGR at careful planning: the use of interior design to produce more satisfactory homes, and open spaces to create a more pleasing environment.

Running off Fountain Street at an angle of 90 degrees were, in parallel, James Street, Frederick Street (completed in 1867-70) and Thomas Street (completed in 1875). These were flanked on one side by Charlemont Square and, on the other, by Fountain Square. James Street and Frederick Street were rapidly built to accommodate the additional workers required during the cotton famine caused by the American Civil War when the linen trade boomed. The houses in James Street were one up, one down, with a small scullery and an enclosed yard with a privy. Those in Frederick Street had two bedrooms. Also built before 1860 were Quarry Row Hill Street and High Street. These were built of stone, were $1\frac{1}{4}$ storeys high and had a squat rural appearance. James Street and Frederick Street had curved felt roofs reminiscent of those at Portlaw. It is suggested that Sophia Malcolmson, when she came as a bride in 1867, asked that these roofs should be incorporated into the village houses to remind her of Portlaw[19].

In the closing decades of the century Thomas Street and College Square were added. College Square later contained a bowling green and was surrounded by workmen's houses 'of superior class each with a trim garden in front and large vegetable garden at the rear'. Numbers 1-23 College Square East were completed in 1882 and numbers 1-12 College Square North, in 1890. In the final years of the century Derrymore Terrace and Maydown Terrace were added. Large semi-detached houses with walled front gardens were provided for managerial staff at Lake View, where they overlooked an artificial lake created to serve the mill. These distinctly middle-class homes had the additional privacy of an avenue.

During the four decades after the establishment of the Bessbrook Mill nearly 700 houses were built and in 1890 the population of the village numbered some 3000, while the company employed some 4500 people at Bessbrook and at its other factories. At that time Bessbrook had its own gas, manufactured on the estate, in addition to a temperance hotel, an institute and a post office. The firm's three hundred-acre farm provided both additional employment and pure milk, often unobtainable in the larger industrial centres.

Bessbrook was linked with Newry by an electric tram, of which there were only two in Ireland. (The other was at Portrush in Co. Antrim and linked the town with the Giant's Causeway). The tram had several interesting features including an arrangement by which goods wagons without flanged wheels ran on a rail lower than that of the passenger wagons, thus allowing them to be towed by horses through the streets at either end of the line. Electricity for the tramway was generated at Millvale, about one mile from Bessbrook. By 1890 the tramway was issuing some 80,000 tickets annually and was the chief means of transport between Bessbrook and Newry[20].

The range of facilities existing in the village was far in advance of what might have been found in contemporary villages and small towns. In 1886-7 the workers petitioned the management for the provision of a community centre. The Institute subsequently built in College Square bears the motto 'In essentials unity, in nonessentials liberty, in all things, charity'. The Institute functioned as a recreational and social centre for the village and was equipped with library, a coffee room, reading room, billiard room and lecture room with accommodation for almost 1000 people.

Bessbrook also possessed a savings bank and a co-operative store in addition to its temperance hotel. Taking advantage of the provisions made for the half-time system of schooling by the Factory Act of 1844, a school was provided as early as 1850. Records indicate the name of J. G. Richardson as manager of a school shared by Roman Catholic and Protestant children - an unusual feature for the period and for that part of Ireland. A newly built schoolhouse had been erected with three schoolrooms comprising a total area of 1260 square feet (Commissioners of Education, 1850). Two teachers, one male and one female, were employed and 66 pupils were enrolled. School hours were 9.30 am-1.30 pm and evening school was from 6.30-8.30 pm[21]. In the following year the Commissioners received an application for an additional salary for the evening school; the application notes that nearly all the pupils were 'adult', many being aged around 18 years. The following year education appears on the books of the factory as an expense. Later in the century the school was enlarged and in 1875 there were 181 pupils, of whom 78 were half-timers in the mill. Sport was encouraged and the firm provided facilities for cricket, rugby and football in addition to a tennis court which was laid out in Charlemont Square. For four consecutive seasons from 1885 the Provincial Towns' Rugby Cup was won by Bessbrook and a number of its players gained international caps.

In view of the religious polarization which is a feature of Northern Ireland, it is interesting to note that Bessbrook enjoyed good community relations. 'Bessbrook typescript' contains an analysis of the workforce in 1901 and reveals that in that year Roman Catholics represented approximately 53% of the workforce followed by Church of Ireland 25% and Presbyterians 20%. Although the population in the surrounding countryside was sharply polarized, JGR initiated a policy designed to create an environment in which those of different religions could co-exist satisfactorily, not an easy task, especially during the Home Rule agitation in the 1880s. He noted that during the 40 years preceding 1886 there was 'an unmistakable increase of friendly feeling and reciprocity between Protestants and Roman Catholics' and that he himself had always 'looked on bigotry with disapproval and encouraged unsectarian education'[22].

An analysis of the 1901 census shows that among the hackers, roughers, flax dressers, spinners and weavers of Thomas Street and Fountain Street there was a good mix of Presbyterian, Roman Catholic and Church of Ireland tenants. The smaller houses in Frederick Street and James Street were mainly occupied by Roman Catholics with some members of Protestant denominations; the more salubrious houses of College Square were almost all occupied by Presbyterians and Church of Ireland tenants[23].

Careful planning was not restricted to the physical lay-out of the village. Methods of social control were as carefully planned, with Richardson adamantly opposed to the introduction of pubs, pawnshops and police into Bessbrook, a prohibition which he was able to maintain without aggressive opposition. Indeed there is some evidence that the temperance policy at Bessbrook was supported by the majority of its inhabitants.

William Allen FRS and his influence on Irish Quakers

It is likely that some of Malcolmson's ideas concerning industrial and social development were influenced by Robert Owen's New Lanark settlement and by Quaker ideas of social improvement then in vogue. In mid-October 1826 Malcolmson received as a visitor to Portlaw Owen's partner and distinguished Quaker scientist, William Allen, since 1801 a Fellow of the Linacre Society and, since 1807, a Fellow of the Royal Society. Allen visited Portlaw on his way south from Belfast where he had been 'most kindly and hospitably received by

James N. Richardson and his wife'. Allen, whose mother came from Cork, had been in an unhappy partnership with Bentham and Owen at New Lanark since 1814. Differences arose concerning the management of New Lanark and of the moral principles to be followed there. Allen objected to Owen's educational ideas and to the curriculum followed in the schools and he became increasingly concerned at Owen's 'vocal infidelity'. Following numerous disputes Owen withdrew from the partnership in 1829; Allen remained involved until 1835.

Allen was a distinguished and highly influential social reformer and social planner. In 1818 he travelled through Sweden, Finland and Russia and saw the Tsar Alexander I at St Petersburg before moving on to Moscow, Odessa and Constantinople, returning to Britain via Italy and France. He travelled widely, interviewing royalty in Prussia and Spain, visiting schools and prisons and promoting his ideas concerning social reform. In 1822 at Vienna he again saw the Tsar Alexander, with whom he had established a close friendship. A long-standing friend of William Wilberforce, Allen established the journal, *The Philanthropist* in 1811 and this became the vehicle for discussing his many schemes for social improvement. New Lanark was 'our great experiment'[24]. In an address to his workpeople he said:

> We are aiming not merely to promote the comfort and happiness of the people of New Lanark but to afford an example to the manufacturers of Glasgow, Stockport, Manchester and in fact to every manufactory [sic] in the whole world for these principles are of universal application ... *the eyes of the world are upon us* [emphasis added][25].

One of Allen's principal interests in his later years was the establishing of what he called an 'agricultural colony' with industrial schools which he helped to found at Lindfield in Sussex. It is likely that David Malcolmson had been acquainted with Allen and his writings, prior to Allen's visit in 1826. Allen, a distinguished Quaker, had been in Ireland attending Quaker meetings in Dublin in 1820 and in 1822 (when he met J. N. Richardson) and it is likely that, on visits to relatives in Cork, he had previously met the Malcolmsons. His visits to Ireland continued and in 1834 he attended the Quaker Yearly Meeting in Dublin. In 1836 he again returned, sailing from Bristol to Cork to visit a government-sponsored agricultural experiment at Pobble O'Keefe not far from Killarney about which he commented 'the plan seems to be to form farms of 60-100 acres ... the results of experiments made upon 300 acres of the bog are delightful'. Allen deplored the fact, however, that no attempt had been made to provide allotments for poor people[26]. On this trip, he again visited James N. Richardson at Lambeg, near Lisburn.

James Grubb Richardson and his motivation towards social improvement

By 1845 the Richardsons had had several decades of experience as employers. JGR lived in Belfast and would have been well aware of the impoverished social conditions of the new urban poor and of the disease, alcoholism, high levels of infant mortality and absenteeism often associated with industrializion. Believing in the benefits of rural surroundings, and also, no doubt, keen to develop an efficient and competent workforce, JGR determined to locate his firm's new factory in the countryside. Richardson papers in the Public Record Office in Belfast provide an insight into the character and motivation of the founder of Bessbrook. JGR explained the reasons for locating his factory at Bessbrook as follows:

> I had a great aversion to be responsible for a factory population in a large town so on looking around we fixed on a place near Newry ... with water power and a thick population around and in a country district where flax was cultivated in considerable quantities[27].

Richardson's concern for the welfare of his workers is revealed in another statement concerning the virtues of the Bessbrook location which also reveals his strength of his purpose and interest in social control:

> It had moreover the desirable condition in my sight of enabling us to control our people and to do them good in every sense.

His paternalism and determination as a social engineer show Richardson as a man of his age. Like Owen, he was no democrat. As the child of Quaker parents who were substantial employers of labour, Richardson possessed a strong sense of responsibility as an employer and he later wrote:

> from childhood I was strongly impressed with the duty we owe to God in looking after the welfare of those around us ... I had long resolved that we should have a temperance population in our little colony[28].

JGR's interest in social improvement was not limited to his experiment at Bessbrook. Ireland was, and remains, a predominantly rural society and economy. Richardson was aware that appropriate models of community must be found for rural society. In the 1860s he took over an extensive estate at the Quaker settlement at Moyallon in Co. Armagh. He was also a benevolent employer who, in the slump of the 1880s, reduced the rents of his tenants when other landowners with estates in Co. Armagh refused to allow any such reduction. A surviving fragment of a letter addressed to him provides an insight into the intellectual and moral atmosphere which characterized Richardson and his contemporaries. It also reveals how the twin priorities of social improvement and economic efficiency were balanced within a framework of paternalistic social control. Moreover, it shows how Quakers were concerned to demonstrate the way forward at a national level as regards social improvement and economic development:

> ... make thy estates at Moyallon *model estates.* Comfortable habitations, neat gardens, good fences, good farming, moral and religious influences in the household, fair wages for the labourers ... all these conditions to be firmly yet lovingly enforced on tenants and on labourers.

> Perhaps more real good might be done, more influence exerted in a national point of view and upon the masses than even Bessbrook - with all its blessings - because *Bessbrook must be the exception* and agriculture *must be the rule.* And I am sure it *would* pay [original emphasis][29].

JGR had one of his homes at The Woodhouse, near Bessbrook. Although he normally lived at Moyallon his influence pervaded every aspect of affairs at Bessbrook and he maintained a keen interest in the village to the end of his life. He developed other business interests and, like the Malcolmsons, became involved in shipping and took an active part in founding the transatlantic Inman Line. However, during the Crimean war when its ships began to carry ammunition to the front he retired from the company on the grounds that, as a member of the Society of Friends, he could not conscientiously be associated with the war. He participated with John Bright in the successful scheme for unsectarian national education in Ireland. In 1882 he was offered a baronetcy by Gladstone but he declined to accept it on the basis that

> I belong to the Society of Friends some of whose members in early days resigned their titles for conscience sake. I cannot say I feel as

strongly as they did ... but I feel as if the acceptance of your offer on the grounds of having tried to do a little for the benefit of my fellow men would detract from the satisfaction I have found in so doing[30].

William Godwin, Robert Owen and the intellectual context of social improvement in the early nineteenth century

What were some of the influences which may have shaped the social philosophy of these early Irish industrialists and social planners? Each would have been aware of the intractable controversy with Owen surrounding New Lanark and both are likely to have shared William Allen's repudiation of Owen's ideas concerning the perfectibility of man by social actions. J. Passmore[31] explores the Lockeian origins of Owen's thought and examines Godwin's redefinition of perfectionism to express the concept of improvement. In the 1796 edition of *Political Justice*, Godwin wrote that:

the term *perfectible* seems sufficiently adapted to express the faculty of being continually made better and receiving perpetual improvement.

There is, Owen wrote,

such a thing as perfecting men, bringing about moral improvement and such a thing as perfectibility, the capacity of being morally improved.

Robert Owen's perfectibilist ideas found their full expression in his *The Book of the New Moral World*, addressed to King William IV. Owen's utopianism and optimism are expressed in the book's dedication in which he declared that the time was ripe for a new kind of society. His book, he claimed, opened to the family of man

the means of endless and progressive improvement, physical, intellectual and moral, and of happiness without the possibility of retrogression of assignable limit.

Owen, it seems, held to the older view of perfectibility and his sweeping optimism concerning the reform of human nature as well as the human condition strikes today's reader as curiously naive. Allen, and presumably Malcolmson and Richardson, would have rejected Owen's views on theological grounds arising from the Biblical view or original sin, received via Augustine and John Calvin and the Scots Quaker, Robert Barclay (see below). But they maintained a strong commitment to the possibility of improvement and would have believed, with Owen, in the improving potential of a balanced environment which included good housing and a measure of social planning. Richardson also believed, of course, that the moral atmosphere in their communities was conducive to encouraging Christian commitment among the workers, though it must be added that Richardson's religious tolerance of the range of Protestant denominations and his cooperation with the Roman Catholic authorities was well known.

Within a tightly knit group such as the Quakers, closely attached as they were to a body of theological and moral principles, the twin ideas of their distinctiveness from the rest of society and of a social mission were very strong. From 1656 Quaker monthly meetings, and later the Society itself, offered criticism and advice, general and particular, on social and business practice. Because they were dissenters many professions were closed to them and their moral principles precluded involvement in many lines of business. They were not interested in buying into the aristocracy and generally followed a relatively frugal lifestyle; consequently they had considerable surplus wealth to re-invest or to channel into improving the social conditions of their workers.

Allen's philosophy of improvement, drawing on a legacy of Quaker thinking about community going back to Bellers and forged in the heat of his conflict with Owen, involved providing conditions in which the lives of employees could be improved in both a social and a spiritual sense. His ideas are developed in his book, *Colonies at Home* (1826 and 1828), of which he sent copies far and wide to his many correspondents including Maria Edgeworth, the Anglo-Irish novelist, and Prince Alexander Galitzin in Russia. Foreshadowing later reformers, he wrote

> The mixture of agriculture and manufacture, I have no doubt, makes the happiest system for the people and whether this tended most to the riches of a state or not, the balance of comfort and happiness would decide a friend of humanity in its favour[32].

It is likely that, as part of their fund of Quaker history, Malcolmson and Richardson would have known of the industrial development at Coalbrookdale in Shropshire by Abraham Darby II and his son-in-law, Richard Reynolds, nicknamed 'The Philanthropist' in the first decade of the eighteenth century[33,34]. The writings of E. Gibbon Wakefield also formed part of the intellectual environment of early nineteenth century Quakers. Wakefield, an associate of J. S.

Mill, was a member of the South Australia Association and of the National Colonization Society which existed from 1830-44. His influential views were frequently published in the *The Spectator* and for two decades from 1829 he published widely on the theory of colonization. Other books by Wakefield which were widely circulated were *A letter from Sydney*, (1829), published under the pen-name Robert Gouger, *The Art of Colonization in England and America*, (London, 1833), and *A View of the Art of Coloniation*, (1849).

Quakers and the temperance movement in Ireland

Bessbrook was established as a temperance community and Richardson's enthusiasm for temperance, and his vigilance, ensured that it remained so until his death in 1890. Founded a generation earlier, Portlaw antedated the full flow of temperance enthusiasm in Ireland. Such was the importance of the temperance element in the development of these communities that it is necessary briefly to explore some of the roots of the movement in Ireland and to indicate in particular the Quaker contribution to its development.

From William Penn to Rowntree, Quakers have written about alcohol abuse and its social effects[35]. Penn wrote about temperance (meaning self-control and moderation), in consumption of food and drink[36]. It was not until the 1830s that temperance came to be associated strictly with alcohol. The Irish temperance movement was born in the winter of 1828-9 at New Ross, Co. Wexford in a Quaker Meeting House and it spread rapidly in the following year. Its main advocate was William Martin, an elderly Quaker shopkeeper living in Cork, who was a governor of the House of Industry together with Father Theobald Mathew. Martin prevailed on Mathew to preach first temperance, and after 1836, abstinence, and under Mathew's leadership a mass movement grew up which became the most striking social mass movement in nineteenth century Ireland[37]. Although Portlaw was not in its beginnings a temperance community, by the early 1840s the movement had taken firm hold and James Stuart, Factory Inspector reported that 'The workers adhere strictly to the Temperance System of Father Mathew'[38].

Though not in earlier life an abstainer, Richardson became a strong believer in the principles of temperance. He resolved that temperance would be one of the guiding principles in the devlopment of his social experiment and at his death was president of the Irish Temperance League[39]. Resolving that Bessbrok should be a temperance village and that there should be no public house, he pursued his policies with energy and determination. Jane N. Richardson records an anecdote concerning women who came from the mountains bringing 'poteen', a dangerous and highly potent native whisky concealed in baskets under calicoes, tapes and ribbons. JGR became aware of this and accosted those whom he suspected of carrying poteen into the village[40]. Bessbrook was widely known in temperance circles and was highly praised by temperance writers of the time including J. Ewing Ritchie, (1878), who wrote a detailed and laudatory study[41].

Possible influences Irish influences on Bournville

It is difficult to determine the extent to which the themes, ideas and developments considered in this paper influenced Quaker thinking in England at the end of the nineteenth century. It has certainly been claimed that Cadbury was influenced in his development of Bournville by the experience of the Richardsons at Bessbrook. The origin of the suggestion, according to a contemporary member of the family, John S. W. Richardson, is as follows. In the autumn of 1921 James N. Richardson of Bessbrook (son of JGR) was ill at Malvern a short time before his death. R. N. Stephen Richardson (the son-in-law of JGR) was visiting him. On a Sunday morning at the Friends' meeting, R. H. S. Richardson met George Cadbury who had a home nearby, and Cadbury told him that

> he had been encouraged by the success of Bessbrook to go ahead with Bournville. What GC's exact words were I don't know. This conversation probably got no further as far as GC was concerned but always remained important in my Father's mind[42].

Whether Cadbury was simply 'encouraged' to go ahead at Bournville by his knowledge of the success of Bessbrook, or whether the influences ran deeper is impossible to establish. What is certain is that the social experiment at Bournville had a distinguished lineage among Irish Quakers.

To review the development of these Irish Quaker industrial communities leads one to reflect on the intellectual and moral ideas, assumptions and ideals, to say nothing of the complex motivations, which might have guided Malcolmson and JGR. Naturally these would have included, as a high priority, interest in economic efficiency. Related to that, however, was a strong interest in ideal communities and in the idea of perfectionism which was an important strand in the intellectual history of the time. Both men were magnificently successful as entrepreneurs. Whatever their paternalism and autocracy, each was regarded widely as a benevolent employer. There is no doubt that the social conditions at Portlaw and Bessbrook were greatly in advance of other industrial settlements in Ireland. Notwithstanding differences in orientation and temperament, the two men, it seems, shared certain principles and assumptions. In addition to their powerful commitment to productivity and to economic efficiency each sought to better the working conditions, and the wider lives, of his employees. Each had a commitment to an ideal of community, and the image of the caring society was promoted at Bessbrook through the provision of various social welfare measures including high-standard housing, medical care, subsidized education, a savings bank and a cooperative store. In the Northern Irish context an important element of this concept of the ideal community was the cultivation of an atmosphere of tolerance and mutual respect between Catholics and Protestants. Of the two men, Richardson was the more ardent exponent of the virtues of temperance but both saw temperance as an essential element in the development of balanced communities.

Their emphasis on social development echoes contemporary interest by Quakers and others in 'colonies', and indeed there had been an earlier Quaker rural settlement experiment at Glentore, Co. Galway. This was another aspect of the ideal community movement which absorbed much of the intellectual energies of E. Gibbon Wakefield and William Allen. It was continued and developed more fully by Ebenezer Howard in *Tomorrow: a peaceful path to real reform*, reissued in 1902 as *Garden Cities of Tomorrow* and hence influenced the development of the Garden City movement.

Detailed discussion of the theological roots of Quaker motivations lies beyond the scope of this article. Although little is known of David Malcolmson's religious experience or thought, Richardson left some notes of his early life which are reproduced in JMR's *Six Generations of Friends in Ireland*[43]. He records the early spiritual influence of J. J. Gurney, Elizabeth Fry and Stephen Grellet, an English Quaker of French Huguenot extraction who was a close friend of William Allen and who accompanied Allen on his visits to Tsar Alexander in London and St Petersburg. One notes in Richardson's reminiscences the compelling sense of Christian stewardship and accountability to God which often characterized nineteenth-century Quakers. This strong sense of calling owes much to Quakerism's theological roots in

Calvinism and the doctrinal formulations of Robert Barclay, published as his *Apology for the True Christian Divinity* ... Richardson's life was characterized by a sense of accountability and of stewardship of time and talents.

Members of local and national Quaker meetings had a very strong sense of group solidarity and identity both within the group and *vis-a-vis* other Quaker groups. Members found it necessary to prove themselves. They were expected to exhibit habits of hard work, thrift, honesty, and scrupulous reliability in trade dealings. As Poggi points out in the context of business occupations 'these habits constituted the characteriological makings of success'; they made the individual credit worthy and led him systematically to re-invest his profits in the business[44].

But, in the case of the Quakers, there was more. They put a high value on their fellow men and women and had strong compassion for the poor. Their commitment to their workers and to the improvement of their circumstances was of equal (and not subordinate) importance to the pursuit of economic efficiency. Surviving private correspondence of JGR provides abundant evidence both of this and of the pride which he took in the general level of the health and fitness of his workers and of their educational and cultural attainments. Writer after writer comments on the favourable conditions at Portlaw and at Bessbrook when compared with other contemporary factory developments. A constant flow of interested and admiring visitors, both non-Quaker and Quaker, must have reinforced the motivation for further social and community development. National awareness of Bessbrook and its reputation and the sense of leading a successful industrial and commercial experiment must have added to Richardson's pride and satisfaction.

The contribution of nineteenth-century Quakers to prison reform, to education, to industry and to the care of the mentally ill is well known. The contribution of Irish Quakers to housing reform and to the development of planning philosophy has not yet been fully recognized. More research is yet needed on the Quaker influences which have helped to shape contemporary notions of community and to guide the course of planning philosophy in Britain.

Acknowledgements

The writer is grateful to the following for their help and suggestions: Mr Gilbert Camblin of Co. Down; Mr S. J. Clewer of Bournville

Village Trust; Professor L. M. Cullen of the University of Dublin, Trinity College; Mrs Olive Goodbody of the Friends' Historical Society, Dublin; Mr Harry Hobson, of Moy, Co. Tyrone; Mr T. Insull of Cadbury Schweppes Ltd; Mr Charles F. Jacob of Waterford; Professor Alan Murie of Heriot Watt University. Thanks are also due to an anonymous referee.

NOTES *

1. J. S. Curl, *European Cities and Society: A Study of the Influence of Political Climate on Town Design*, London: Leonard Hill, 1970, p.141.
2. I. Grubb, *Quakers in Ireland*, 1654-1900, London: The Swarthmore Press, 1927, p.140, 141.
3. C. Fell Smith, *James N. Richardson of Bessbrook*, London: Longman, Green and Co., 1925, p.43.
4. J. Bellers, *Proposals for raising a colledge of industry of useful trades and husbandry*, London: T. Sowle, 1695, reprinted in 1817, (London: R. & A. Taylor) and in 1916, (London: Headley Bros.). K. Marx, *Das Kapital*, 2nd edn Vol. I, p.515. Quoted in W. C. Braithwaite, *The Second Period of Quakerism*, London: Macmillan and Co., 1919, p.571. Robert Barclay, *An Apology for the True Christian Divinity, as the same is held forth and preached by ther People called in scorn Quakers* published in Latin in 1676 and in English in 1678. The fourteenth edition was published by R.B. Murdoch in Glasgow in 1886.

* Note on sources: microfilm notes on the Malcolmson family are held in the National Library of Ireland in Dublin. Malcolmson papers, including a copy of the ledger of Malcolmson Mill, Portlaw, are held in the National Archives, Dublin. Minutes and correspondence of the Bessbrook Spinning Company, 1881-1956 are held in the Public Record Office of Northern Ireland, Belfast. Photographs of Bessbrook in the nineteenth century are held in the Lawrence Collection in the National Library of Ireland and in the Welch and Hogg Collection in the Ulster Museum, Belfast. For some of the above material relating to Bessbrook the writer is indebted to an invaluable, but unidentified, unpublished typescript which includes a study of Bessbrook valuation records and material based on a number of interviews with residents carried out in 1978. For convenience this is referred to as 'Bessbrook typescript'.

5. *Braithwaite, 1919, op. cit.* [7], pp.571-94.
6. G. L. Smith, Ireland: *Historical and Statistical,* (1844-7), p.177.
7. A. N. B. Garvan, Proprietary Philadelphia as an artifact in O. Handlin and J. Burchard (eds), *The Historian and the City,* Cambridge, MA: MIT Press, 1966.
8. Armytage, 1961, *op. cit.* [4], p.31.
9. O. Goodbody, *Guide to Irish Quaker Records,* Dublin: Stationery Office for I.M.C., 1967, p.85, no. 68. For a discussion of Thomas Greer, linen merchant and ancestor of William Malcolmson, see J. W. McConaghy, Thomas Greer, a Quaker linen merchant of Dungannon, 1724-1803, unpublished PhD dissertation, The Queen's University of Belfast, 1979.
10. T. J. Howell, *Report of Factory Inspectors,* 1836, Parliamentary Papaers, 1836, Vol. XLV, p.138.
11. S. Lewis, *Topographical Dictionary,* London: S. Lewis and Co., 1837, p.302.
12. Report of James Stuart, Inspector of Factories, 1842.
13. J. F. Maguire, *The Industrial Movement in Ireland as Illustrated by the National Exhibition of 1852,* Cork: 1853.
14. E. D. Mapother, The unhealthiness of Irish towns and the want of legislation, in *Journal of the Social and Statistical Society of Ireland,* Dubin: 1864, Vol. IV, p.261.
15. C. Gill, *The Rise of the Irish Linen Industry,* Oxford: Oxford University Press, 1964; W. H. Crawford, 'The origins of the linen industry in North Armagh and the Lagan Valley', *Ulster Folklife,* XVII, (1971).
16. S. Lewis, 1837, *op. cit.*
17. G. H. Bassett, *The Book of Armagh,* Dublin: 1888, p.236.
18. H. N. Pym, *Memories of Old Friends being extracts from the journals and letters of Caroline Fox,* 1835-71, London: 1882.
19. Bessbrook typescript, *p.61.*
20. A. T. Newham, *The Bessbrook and Newry Tramway,* Headington, Oxford: Oakwood Press, 1979.
21. Public Record Office of Northern Ireland, Mss. ED1/1/126-9.
22. J. N. Richardson, *Reminiscences of Friends in Ireland,* Gloucestershire: John Bellows, 1912.
23. Bessbrook typescript, *op. cit.*
24. *Life of William Allen,* Vol. 1, London: Charles Gilpin, 1846, p.353.
25. *Ibid.* Vol. 1, p.349.
26. *Ibid.* Vol. II, p.237.
27. J. N. R., *Six Generations of Friends in Ireland,* 1655-1890, (3rd edn), 1895, p.228.

28. Anon., [Thomas Adams], Bessbrook: A Record of Industry in a Northern Ireland Village Community and of a Social Experiment, Belfast: Richardson, Sons and Owden, 1945, p.31.
29. Grubb letter, 1863. Archives of the Friends' Historical Society, Dublin.
30. J. G. Richardson to W. E. Gladstone, 24 April 1882; reproduced in Anon. [Thomas Adams], 1945.
31. J. Passmore, The Perfectibility of Man, (2nd impression), London: Duckworth, 1971, p.159.
32. Life of William Allen, London: Charles Gilpin, 1846, p.431f.; see also, entry on William Allen in Dictionary of National Biography.
33. I. Grubb, Quakerism and Industry before 1800, London: Williams and Norgate, 1930.
34. A. Raistrick, Quakers in Science and Industry, Newton Abbot: David and Charles, 1968, p.136f.
35. J. Rowntree, (various editions), The Temperance Problem and Social Reform, London: Hodden and Stoughton, (1899-1901).
36. W. Penn, Collected works of William Penn, London: The Assign of J. Sowie, 1726, pp.341-4, 366, 372, 823, 854.
37. E. Malcolm, Ireland Sober, Ireland Free: Drinking and Temperance in Nineteenth Century Ireland, Dublin: Gill and Macmillan, 1986.
38. Parliamentary Papers, Report of James Stuart, for half year ending 31 December 1842.
39. J. G. Richardson, obituary, Illustrated London News, 3 May 1890; The Manufacture of Linen at Bessbrook Warehousemen and Drapers' Trade Journal, 29 March 1890, pp.297-302.
40. J. N. Richardson, *Bessbrook and its Linen Mills: A short narrative of a model temperance town,* London: W. Tweedy and Co., 1878.
41. J. Ewing Ritchie, *Bessbrook and its Linen Mills: A short narrative of a model temperance town,* London: W. Tweedy, 1878.
42. Personal communication from J. S. W. Richardson, 26 March 1975.
43. Richardson, 1893, op. cit. [n], 220f.
44. G. Poggi, *Calvinism and the Capitalist Spirit: Max Weber's Protestant Ethic,* London: 1893, p.77.

BOOK REVIEW

Orange, Green and Khaki: The Story of the Irish Regiments in the Great War, 1914-18 by Tom Johnstone
Dublin: Gill & Macmillan, Dublin 1992, 498pp. £17.99

One's first impression of this book is its fine presentation. There are good maps at the front and a glossary indicating military ranks, honours awards etc.

Having noted the above I turned to the chapter headings and the illustrations. From this I confess, without shame, that a sense of horror engulfed me. "Here we go again," I said to myself. Loos, the Somme, Passchendaele, Suvla Bay, Salonika. A war of attrition with fruitless, badly conceived and executed plans to turn the flanks. Close to a million men from the British Empire; well over a million from France and three million from Germany and Austria-Hungary - all dead.

Fifty-five years ago when I started Military History attention was focused on the factual events of World War One. Much less consideration was given to the sordid and horrifying human and social factors. Perhaps it was too close to the actual event.

Johnstone's book relates with considerable sensitivity the stories of courage, tribulation and at times deplorable leadership at the highest level. It also reminds one, very fairly, of the dilemma into which all ranks of these famous regiments were placed. It is epitomised on page 17 where as the British Expeditionary Force (BEF) marched forward to Mons in August 1914 they were greeted by the French with, 'Vivent les Anglais.' The Irish replied, 'Nous ne sommes pas Anglais. Nous sommes Irlandais'. (We are not English we are Irish.) The reader should ponder deeply on this response.

Johnstone succinctly comments that 'the Irish had a contempt for danger bordering on the reckless'. There was also a traditional, easy affinity between officers and men in an Irish Regiment which before then was quite rare although more common throughout the Army in World War Two and since'' it is sad to point out that Irishmen who had specifically enlisted in Irish Regiments of their choice should find themselves drafted to serve with English and Scottish Regiments.

For those purely interested in the history of World War One this is a highly readable book. Tom Johnstone has done an immense amount of research and is to be congratulated on having written such a studied work.

Charles R Irwin
Major (retired) late Royal Northumberland Fusiliers
LL.B., FCIS., MIL

BOOK REVIEW

A History of the Parish of St Joseph's, Hannahstown, Co. Antrim 1826-1993, Detailing the Names of the Graves in the Old Graveyard, by Eileen Fulton. Ulster Journals Ltd. 1993. 74pp £5.

Local studies of the community can make a vital contribution to the sense of continuity that is sorely lacking in areas such as West Belfast. Eileen Fulton's *History of the Parish of St Joseph's* not only goes some of the way towards filling the gap but, as an example of the value of linking local history studies with the transcription of gravestones, is in itself a model for others to follow.

Her record of the names on gravestones is supplemented by the benefits of her local knowledge and historical research. The names are often accompanied by her own or communal recollections of notable individuals or by pen-portraits based on her research in parish records or local libraries. The sections on the history of the original St Joseph's parish which trace its development from the Penal Era, and that of the more recent St Teresa's parish from 1911, are complemented by an annotated list of 'priests whose remains are buried in Hannahstown Graveyard' and by illustrations of priests and local buildings of historical merit (including Turf Lodge Farm, her own home).

This book is inspirational in another sense: Eileen Fulton's dedication to the importance of the task she had set herself and her determination to see it published were strong enough to sustain her through a crippling and ultimately fatal illness, borne with great courage and dignity.

Trevor Parkhill

BOOK REVIEW

An introduction to Irish Research. Irish Ancestry: A Beginner's Guide
by Bill Davis (Federation of Family History Society, 1992)

A recent review article in *Familia* suggested that, like the farmer and
the cowboy, the historian and the genealogist should be friends,
contending that there was much to be gained from greater
co-operation. Where stands the archivist in this pow-wow, when he is
not waging a war-dance against both? There have been a number of
'introductions' to genealogical research in Ireland, of which this title is
a worthy, if limited, example. Without exception they all would have
been improved immeasurably by closer consultation with the curators
of records which are recommended for readers.

The necessarily short descriptions of sources are sufficient as far
as they go. They are almost exclusively concerned, however, with the
post 1850 period. Most archivists in Ireland would lay a quiet bet that
the great majority of serious inquirers would be able to trace their
search back as far as the 1850s. It is the pre-Griffith Valuation period
which, in view of the absolute dearth of census and relative scarcity of
church registers, considerably increases the degree of difficulty of
source-based family research. Information about the availability of
eighteenth- and seventeenth- century estate, tax and private records
would help genealogists to be aware of the possibilities of taking their
search an important step further. To be fair, this may be the aim of the
second volume which the blurb says is in preparation, though it would
in that case be helpful to know what will be included in its eventual
publication.

Successful searches for Irish ancestors depend to a great extent on
the ability to 'only connect' between the sources that are available.
This requires the sort of explanatory detail that archivists concern
themselves with and which is found in introductory texts to sources in
their care. Greater use of this expertise would help searchers to
compensate for deficiencies in the availability of records, not least by
knowing to which alternative sources they might turn. The outcome
would be better-informed searchers asking more purposeful questions
of the curators of sources.

This publication avoids many but not all of the pitfalls of research
in Ireland. Denominational differences in church records are restricted
to 'Roman Catholic' and 'Protestant'. The failure to differentiate

between the various Protestant religions' most blatantly Presbyterianism, Methodist and Society of Friends, masks an important range of sources of proven genealogical value and could mislead researchers about a crucial aspect of their research, the religious affiliation of their forebears. In the 'census substitutes' section reference to the value of school registers, available from the 1860s, would have acknowledged recent writings on the subject. Inaccuracies and omissions are inevitable, but it is curious that there is no mention of the Irish Genealogical Project, an island-wide co-operative venture, in which archivists are involved in an advisory role, to put on computer entries from church registers of all denominations with the specific aim of helping visitors who arrive in Ireland to research their ancestors, the declared intention of this publication.

Trevor Parkhill

NOTES ON CONTRIBUTORS

Flann Campbell, son of the Ulster poet Joseph Campbell, was born in 1919. He has written extensively on education and historical matters. His most recent book *The Dissenting Voice: Protestant Democracy in Ulster from plantation to partition* (Blackstaff Press, Belfast, 1991) received much critical acclaim. He now lives in Blackrock, Co. Dublin.

Winifred Glover is Keeper of Ethnography in the Ulster Museum, Belfast, and has published widely in the areas of her special subject and in local history and genealogical journals, including *Familia* (1987).

Rev. Dr. Ambrose MacAuley is parish priest of St. Brigid's Roman Catholic Church, Belfast. The article which appears here was originally given as the 1990 Canon Rogers Memorial Lecture at St. Mary's College, Belfast, and is one of many by Dr. MacAuley on ecclesiastical history. His publications include *Dr Russell of Maynooth* (Darton Longman and Todd, London, 1983); *Patrick Dorrian, Bishop of Down and Connor, 1865-85* (The Academic Press, Dublin, 1987). His William Crolly, Archbishop of Armagh will be published by Four Courts Press, Dublin (Spring, 1994)

Trevor McClaughlin is an Ulster man teaching history at Macquarie University, Sydney, NSW, Australia. His main publications on Irish–Australian links are *From Shamrock to Wattle: digging up your Irish Ancestors* (Collins, Sydney, 1985). *Barefoot and Pregnant: Irish famine orphans in Australia* (The Genealogical Society of Victoria, 1991). His article on the latter subject was also published in Familia (1987)

Arthur Williamson lectures in the Department of Social Administration and Policy at the University of Ulster at Coleraine and has wide research interests in 19th and 20th century administration in Ireland. An earlier version of the article published here appeared in *Planning Perspectives* (1992).

IRISH MANUSCRIPTS COMMISSION
NEW BOOKS

William Herbert's Croftus Sive de Hibernia liber   £25.00IR

Latin text with English translation giving a view of Ireland and Munster in particular in the 1590's. eds. John A. Madden and Arthur Keaveney

Analecta Hibernica No. 35   £25.00IR

includes text of a rare Catholic Jacobite pamphlet with wide ranging proposals for agricultral improvements in Ireland, c. 1698.

Crown Surveys of Lands 1540-41   £40.00IR

with the Kildare Rental begun in 1518. ed. Gearoid MacNiocaill

Vol. 1, Calendar of Exchequer Inquisitions: 1455-1699. £50.00IR

ed. Margaret Griffith (1991), pp xviii + 769

This is the first volume in a series providing summaries in English extracted from 32 volumes of Calendars of Inquisitions in Latin and 42 vols. of deeds and wills in the Irish Record Commission collection. The originals of these documents mainly dealing with property in Cos. Dublin, Wicklow, Meath and Kildare were destroyed in 1922

Calendar of Material relating to Ireland in   £40.00IR
the High Court of Admiralty Examinations, 1536-1641.

ed. John Appleby, pp xxi + 375

Forthcoming

Calendar of Papal Letters relating to Great Britian and Ireland Vol. XVII: Alexander VI pt II 1498-1503, ed. Anne P. Fuller

Calendar of Rosse Papers, Birr Castle. A.P.W. Malcomson

Court of Claims: submissions and evidence 1663. Geraldine Tallon

Memoranda Roll of the Irish Exchequer 3 Edward II. David Craig

Analecta Hibernica No. 36

Calendars of State Papers, Ireland, 1509-85

This series to be published by HMSO London is a joint project of the Irish Manuscripts Commission and the Public Record Office, London and is under the general editorship of Prof. Nicholas Canny, University College, Galway. The first volume for the years 1509-49, edited by Steven Ellis and James Murray, will be published in 1994.

Orders to: **I.M.C., 73 Merrion Square, Dublin 2.**

If Paying by Credit Card (Access/American Express/Diners Club/Mastercard/ Visa) Please Contact: **Ulster Historical Foundation, 12 College Square East, Belfast BT1 6DD. Tel: (0232) 332288 Fax: (0232) 239885**

UNIVERSITY OF ULSTER
PROGRAMME OF SHORT COURSES
FOR OVERSEAS STUDENTS

The University of Ulster has established the Programme of Short Courses for overseas Students specifically to provide academic programmes for students from all parts of the world. Most of the courses take place during the summer period, and many are concerned with the history and culture of Ulster and Ireland. During courses arrangements will be made for participants to undertake visits to places of historic and scenic interest.

In addition to promoting courses of its own, the Programme will cater to the needs of specific groups, and will endeavour to respond to proposals from external bodies and institutions suggesting particular short courses.

Courses will take place on one or more of the four campuses of the University of Ulster: Belfast, Coleraine, Jordanstown (near Carrickfergus) and Magee College, Londonderry. Students will normally stay in University Halls of Residence on campus (except Belfast were participants will be accomodated in nearby Jordanstown).

Further information is available from:

The Director
Programme of Short Courses for Overseas Students
University of Ulster
Coleraine
BT52 1SA
Northern Ireland

Telephone +44 265 44141   Extension 4155
Fax +44 265 40930